Zen
and the Ambient Echo
The Psychological Philosophy of Being

Scott Shaw

BUDDHA ROSE PUBLICATIONS

First Edition 2020

ISBN 10: 1-949251-23-3
ISBN 13: 978-1-949251-23-4

Library of Congress: 743289974

Printed in the United States of America
10 9 8 7 6 5 4 3 2

ZEN AND THE AMBIENT ECHO
THE PSYCHOLOGICAL PHILOSOPHY OF BEING

Introduction

Here it is, *The Scott Shaw Zen Blog 15.0,* originally presented on the *World Wide Web.* All of the writings presented in this book were written between September 2019 and February of 2020.

As was the case with the previously published volumes based upon *The Scott Shaw Zen Blog;* entitled: *Scribbles on the Restroom Wall, The Chronicles: Zen Ramblings from the Internet, Words in the Wind, Zen Mind Life Thoughts, The Zen of Life, Lies, and Aberrant Reality, Apostrophe Zen, and The Abstract Arsenal of Zen and the Psychology of Being, Zen and Again: The Metaphysical Philosophy of Psychology, Tempest in a Teapot and the Den of Zen, Buddha in the Looking Glass, Wo Ton' of the Blue Vision, Zen and the Psychology of the Spiritual Something, Pyrophoric Zen, Fragments of Paradox, and Zen: Traversing the Entity of Non-Entity,* this volume is presented exactly as it was viewed on *scottshaw.com* with no rewriting, punctuation, or typo corrections. From this, we hope you will receive the original reading experience.

This volume of internet ramblings is presented with the date and time listed as to when each blog was originally posted. Also, the blogs in this volume are presented from last to first. With this, we hope to present a transcendence back through time as opposed to an evolving evolution. In addition, we left out the traditional *Table of Contents* in an attempt to leave this volume with a much more free-flowing reading experience.

Okay, there's the information and the definitions. Read on... We hope you enjoy it. And, be sure to stayed tuned for the ongoing *Scott Shaw Zen Blog @ scottshaw.com.*

Translating words from an ancient language like Sanskrit is always a bit tricky. Languages are developed to reflect the culture, the temperament, and the mindset of a specific place and a time in history. Stepping back thousands of years and what was going on then is absolutely different from what is going on now.

This is simply a preface to understanding that when you use a word, particularly a word from an ancient culture, its interpretation may vary. But, its essence should remain the same.

The simple translation of the Sanskrit word, *"Daivim,"* is, *"Shining one."* In Sanskrit, the word, *"Daivim,"* is used to describe a person who is the embodiment of positive energy and is moving forwards like a Deva or Devi—a god like creature.

How many people do you know who are truly positive creatures? How many people do you know that consciously form their existence around doing only positive things? How many people do you know that do not hold a self-interest in their interactions with other people? How many people do you know that exist in a space of pure positivity? How about you?

The thing that most people never take the time to think about or even consider is everything that they do is a choice. What they do they do for a reason but more times than not that reason is not based upon a mindset of positivity, that reason is based upon a mindset of self-gratification.

Who do you think is the better person? The individual who is constantly trying to rise up the ladder of life; getting more and having more, or the person who is actually embracing positivity in all that they do and truly spreading that positive energy, without reservation, in all that they do?

In your life, you can make the decision to be positive. You can make the decision to put your own needs and desires on the backburner and step forward through the rest of your life in a selfless manner, doing positive things, and only embracing positive energy. It's not easy, I get it. But, at the end of the day what really matters in the life of any person; them getting what they want, feeding what they believe they deserve or desire in any given moment, or them spreading the positive universal energy of light onto all people and all things?

Life is your choice. You can do whatever you want with it. You can make justifications for all that you do. But, there is only one truth in the ever-expanding, ever-evolving cornucopia of existence and that truth is, the person who chooses to embrace positivity and spread that energy outwards, everywhere is truly understood to be the best and the greatest of what humanity has to offer.

Do you feel bad about telling a lie?

Do you feel bad about whom your lie affected?

What do you do once you have lied?

Do you lie about the lies you have told?

What do you do when you find out that something you believe was a lie?

*　　*　　*

01/Feb/2020 08:35 AM

When somebody steals something from you should they be allowed to keep it?

The question of good or bad—bad or good is all based upon perspective. It is calculated upon the concept of what a specific individual is basing their life decisions upon. It is defined by what one person wants in relation to what someone else wants. Thus, there is no absolute definition of good or bad.

It is very common that people call out the so called, *"Good deeds,"* of someone. It is also common that people call out the, *"Bad actions,"* of someone. But, who draws the lines for these definitions?

If we look around we can see all kinds of bad things going on all the time. People steal from other people. People hit other people. People lie. People kill. People do abstract actions that negativity hurt the life of someone else. People say things that hurt people. But, look at these deeds on the larger scale; is there not always someone out there that cheers on these action(s)? Is there not always someone out there condoning and liking what that someone has done even if what they have done is to do something that is knowingly wrong?

This is the same with people who launch into what may be considered an obviously good deed. The person does what they do in order to help someone. They do what they do for what they believe is the greater good. But, no good deed has universally positive repercussion. Is giving a panhandler money on the street corner so they can by drugs a good thing? Is allowing a homeless person to live wherever they want, while they destroy that neighbor and environment with their waste a good thing? Is stealing something from one person to give to someone else an honorable deed? Is condemning one person because they stand up for their rights an honorable action? The list goes on but just because something may be seen as good does not mean that it will ultimately have an idealist outcome.

Think about something that you have done that has hurt someone. Did you plan what you were about to do? Did you realize it would hurt them? When you were told that you hurt them, how did you feel about that fact? Once you were told that you had hurt someone, did you care about their feelings and what did you do about any of this?

Think about something that you have done that has helped someone. Did you plan what you were about to do? Did you realize it would help them? When you were told that you helped them, how did you feel about that fact? Once you were told that you had helped someone, did you ever take the time to study who you may have hurt in the process of your helping that someone?

Most people operate from a perspective of, *"Me."* They think about themselves first and everyone else second. What they do, whether it may be considered good or bad, they are doing it for the reason that it will provide them with that something that they want. Even the people that do nothing are doing something.

Most people operate from a perspective of doing what they do and then either relish in the rewards or they make excuses for their actions and blame other people or outside causation factors when they are confronted with the fact that they have done something that is considered wrong.

Though there is no final definition for good or for bad, what there is, is the known reality of internal truth. You know if what you are doing is good or bad. You know if what you are doing will hurt someone. You know if what you are doing will help someone. If you look deeply into your being you will also know why you are doing what you are doing and, without a doubt, if you truly study your motivations for you doing anything, you will see that what you are doing you are doing to benefit you.

If YOU is the motivation, is what you are doing good for YOU or is it truly good for someone else?

If YOU is the motivation, is what you are doing bad for YOU or is it bad for someone else?

If you cannot study the Bigger Picture. If you cannot look to the source of your motivations, causing you to do what you do, all that you do will ultimately only come to be understood as Bad and harm you and other people.

Though there is no absolute definition for good or bad there is an absolute definition as to what your action seeking Good or seeking Bad will do to one other person or an entire group of people. If what you do is geared towards or is knowingly going to hurt someone/anyone that action is bad. And, Bad is never a Good thing.

The great mystic, George Ivanovich Gurdjieff created a very powerful meditation technique most commonly known as, *"The Stop Exercise."* In essence, what this meditation technique employs is that someone calls out, *"Stop,"* and this is exactly what you do. You shut it all down. You stop. You stop your body from moving. You stop your mind from thinking.

Once this Stop Exercise has been executed the most essential fact is that you totally Stop. If your eyes are open you do not close them or blink. If your mouth is closed, you do not open it. You completely Stop wherever you find yourself.

Once you have Stopped, it is essential that you immediately note the condition of your body and your mind. You chart how you are standing or sitting. You note how your body is feeling where you find yourself. You observe your mental condition. You check your emotions and note what you are feeling and why. If you can, you allow this Stop to allow you to chart your way down to the sourcepoint of your being.

The Stop exercise also allows you to halt all thoughts in your mind. Stop means Stop thinking. Freeze your mind and become one with the nothingness.

Some say that the Stop Exercise only can work when someone else executes it as this causes you to be forced to Stop when you never expected it. Though the random invocation of someone else calling out, *"Stop,"* is a great meditating motivation, many times all things that may be gained from this exercise will be lost because you do not have anyone to practice it with you. If this is the case, do not let the benefits of the Stop meditation technique go. You can practice it solo. You just have to do it from a space of consciousness where you do not plan to do it at a specific time or place or when you are in a specific state of mind. Do it randomly, when you least expect it. Stop yourself.

Another essential caveat that one can and should take into consideration as a reasoning for employing this meditation exercise is that most people spend much of their lifetime doing things either for themselves and or to or for other people. Meaning, people are either doing things for themselves believing that it will make their life better or happier or they are doing things that either help or hurt other people. Think about your life. Think about the things that you do. If you chart your existence in your mind you will instantly realize that this is true.

The Stop Exercise is a great way to remove yourself from this selfish: helpful or hurtful pattern of living. When you find yourself becoming self involved, Stop. When you find yourself thinking or doing hurtful things, Stop. When you Stop, you Stop. When you have Stopped, nothing else is actualized or damaged and from this karma and life repercussions are ended.

In this modern era, the Stop Exercise does not have to be practiced face-to-face. There are a few people I practice this technique with and we periodically text each other, *"Stop."* Though not as dramatic as someone calling out, *"Stop,"* it definitely can have the same effect.

The Stop Exercise is a great means to force your mind to confront its Now. It causes you, if even for a moment, to move beyond the constrains of everyday reality and move into your meditative mind. From this, all kinds of new levels of realization and internal peace may be encountered.

STOP!

* * *

29/Jan/2020 06:50 AM

Nobody wants to die. Even the people who claim that they want to die really just want a better life.

Have you ever had one of those experiences when you are in a store or a supermarket and you keep bumping into the same person? Wherever you are going that seems to be the same location they are headed. When this happens to me, I usually do something like make the joke, *"We keep getting in each others way,"* or something like that. It's just life. Sometimes some people are looking for the same thing and headed in the same direction.

I was at the supermarket and out of nowhere I hear this woman just going off. *"Stop following me! You've followed me all the way from the parking lot! I'm going to get you arrested! You're a terrorist!"*

What was going on was the lady yelling was this white woman that I would place in her fifties. She was going off on this couple, of middle-eastern descent that were in their thirties. She was going off and she would not stop. I mean she was yelling. The only mistake the couple made is that they let themselves get sucked in. *"We're not following you, you're following us."* It was loud.

With all eyes on the what was going on, the manager steps in. Though one may call his decision a bit racist, he walks the couple away. But, no one was kicked out of the store and their shopping continued. I checked out and left so I don't know if there was any additional confrontation but I do know that some people are just insane and sometimes you are going to have to encounter them.

Once upon a time, in the long ago and the far-far away, I had this one totally insane neighbor that lived next to me for over two years. Years later and I still have not recovered from all the noise and nonsense his uncontrolled insanity put my life through. It really took a toll. On the surface, he was a normal looking guy. Live next to him and you could not help but encounter his insanity.

And, this is the thing about life; sometimes people are just nuts.

On the surface this lady seemed fairly normal. Her hair was combed and her clothing was well put together. But, somewhere inside her mind there was a malfunction. This and/or these malfunctions is what sets the dominos falling in the life of the other people they encounter. And, there probably is no drug for this to fix them up as they are, for the most part, functionally insane. Some small little something-something pushes them to one side, however, and the dysfunctionality kicks in.

Sure, we can all say we're a bit off. Some people even take pride in that. I've known people who have stepped back from the world and became very reclusive due to their being aware of their failing mental health. But, most of the insane are not like that. They simply make excuses (to themselves) for their uncontrolled actions. They justify their conduct. They believe that what they are doing is okay and what that other someone is doing is wrong.

Life is weird. Some people are weird. Some people are simply insane. The more you are in the out-there, the larger your chance of encounter that someone who is just nuts. And, when they come at you they will come at you for no reason. A reason lost only in the depths of their own insanity.

The question to answer... Just walk away...
Don't let them suck you into their insanity.

27/Jan/2020 12:38 PM

What you think about is what you are reminded of.

You want to forget something? Erase all of the reminders.

When All You Have To Do Is Get Naked To Be Famous
27/Jan/2020 08:44 AM

Fame is an interesting animal. The pursuit of fame is a demonic beast. There are certain people who desire fame. Some of these people are willing to do anything to rise to that state. But, what is fame? Why do people pursue fame? What is the cost of gaining fame? What does fame really prove? And, how does fame help anything?

Once upon a time, in the long ago and the far-far away, fame was solely based on an individual's accomplishment of something. One person did one thing that no one else had done and they were rewarded for it. Then came the people who stole or capitalized on the unique creation(s) of other people. Then came the people who became famous by talking or writing about what another person had created. Then came people doing whatever it took to become famous. But, what was and is the price of this fame? And, who pays that price?

As the world moved into the industrial age, there was born various forms of technology that allowed the fame of a person to spread beyond those who encountered that person in person. First there was printing, then photography, then the moving pictures, then the internet. Each new form of technology provided new methods for an individual to find fame. But also, hand-in-hand with each new level of technological expansion fueling the fame machine, the morality of what was understood to be good, wholesome, and whole diminished.

Certainly, the nude form has been depicted and admired since the dawning of art and particularly painting. Painting requires technique, however. Painting requires talent. Painting witnesses the artist first seeking and then finding their vision and then discovering a way to place it upon a canvas. This is not something that could be done by anyone. This is what set the artist apart from the masses. This is also what caused them to find fame in a deserving manner.

As technology moved forward, the use of the human form shifted from the artist to the model. With photography and later moving pictures it was the person posing who predominately found their way to fame and not the person who captured that image. Thus, finding fame became much easier. All a person had to do was take off their clothing.

A beautiful woman—a woman willing to be naked in front of the camera, equaled men, who have no other release, flocking to their images and hailing their name. Fame, yes. But, fame at what cost? And, fame solely for the sake of fame. …Fame that was not based in any unique or meaningful contribution to the ever-growing reality of human consciousness.

Pretty, beautiful, invigorating; sure. But, enlightening? No.

This is the same with those who ride on the coattails of the true artists, the true visionaries, and the true creators. They do this by various methods but the defining factor of them verses the artists and the creators is that they did not instigate or actualize what they are discussing. They were not the sourcepoint. Yet, in many cases, some of them find more fame then the individual who actually deserves the fame.

This brings us to the question, why do some people wish to become famous?

First of all, if a person is creating something unique and their own, they may deserve fame. Thus, fame may simply find its way to them in a deserving manner. That is one example. But, then there is the person who simply desires fame. Maybe they believe they are beautiful, talented, or whatever... But, they have done nothing unique. They have created nothing new or moved any previously created medium forward to a new level of suchness. They simply want fame. But, why do they or anybody else seek fame? The answer is really quite simple. They are not whole onto themselves. They are not self-aware. They are looking outside of themselves to gain something that is lacking inside of themselves and, thus, they believe by finding people who like them, (at whatever cost), they will not feel so empty.

From this, is born all of the people who seek fame, simply as fame, and have not earned it. They associate with those who are famous. They talk about those who are famous. They take off their clothing and allow people to look at their body simply as a means to be thought of as appealing. But, fame that is not deserved—that is born and then borrowed from the vision(s) and creation(s) of someone else is undeserved fame. And, just like the female who was once young, fit, and beautiful and found her fame by getting naked, any fame gained by the person who created nothing unique will all fade with the passing of time leaving that individual more empty and more pursuant then they were when they began to walk down the pathway of obtaining undeserved fame.

Freedom is simple. Be free and you are free. If you are in need of finding fame, if you are in need of seeking the approval and admiration of others to heal the holes in your being, you should first find a road to self-knowledge and self-realization instead of following a pathway that leads you to something that you did not earn and/or do not deserve.

Back in the seventies, when I was first going to college, I lived at this apartment that was adjacent to the L.A. River. ...Right next to it, in fact. It was kind of strange, really... Everyday when I drove to my parking spot in the back of the building, I would parallel the L.A. River but unless it was very full due to a very heavy rain, I didn't think that much about it.

For those of you who may not know, the L.A. River is not really a river in the truest/purest sense. It is a cement walled structure that runs for miles upon miles through the L.A. Basin. But, everyday it serves a purpose. A purpose that few people, including myself back then, rarely thought/think about.

Back then, one of my forms of transportation was a Yamaha 350 motorcycle. They were quite the rage then. It was orange. I bought it from a former *Hari Krishna* who was living in Laguna Beach. Back then, you paid the price of the cc's for a used motorcycle. Thus, I paid $350.00 for it.

I used to love scooting around on it. Back then, there was no helmet law and riding it was a really freeing experience.

I was very involved in the formalized aspects of yoga and spirituality at that point in my life. I was never a good university student, I preferred to spend my time involved with living the spiritual path. I spent a lot of time at my teacher *Swami Satchidananda's Integral Yoga Institute.*

Swamji, as we called him back then, used to drive this gigantic old-school Cadillac. Long before the term old-school was even invented. Yes, a Swami driving a Cadillac. But, I won't get into that here. It was like a 1962 totally resorted piece of rolling automotive history.

One day, as I was jamming down the 101 freeway on my motorcycle, shooting between the clogged cars in the afternoon traffic jam, I saw Swamji's Cadillac up ahead. Though I didn't really slow down as I zipped passed him, I did give him and his passenger a wave.

Of course, they knew who I was. More importantly, I was coming from school so I had my backpack on. It was a blue daypack made by North Face. But, more importantly, I had a photo pin of Swami Satchidananda attached to it. It was my way, at that time, of letting the world know where my mind was at.

School is often a time of expressing who you are and what you like. Though times have changed a lot, I remember how people would write things like the name of the bands they liked on their *Pee Chee* folder and stuff like that. Back in the lunch box days, people would carry a lunch box depicting their favorite TV show... You probably remember similar things... Back in Junior High I had a Peter Max notebook. I was always into art.

Anyway... I don't know what happened to that pin. But, it is gone. I look for them on eBay every now and then but they never seem to be offered. Maybe they are gone forever? I do not know. A symbol of a time gone past.

Soon after that motorcycle pass-by, at a lecture of Swami Satchidanand's that I was doing the sound and running the tapes recorders for, Gurudev looked over at me while mentioning how dangerous motorcycles were. I should have listened.

A year or so later I had a life changing motorcycle accident.

…We are always warned about the things to come, we just have to be open enough to listen.

The point of all this… We each project who were are or at least who we think we are and how we want to be seen by the world. What we wear, how we do our hair, the car we do drive or do not drive, and the pins we put on our backpacks are all a depiction of how we want the world to see us.

Think about yourself. Is there ever a day that you walk outside that you don't first consider what you are wearing or how your hair is combed and stuff like that?

Some people are very obsessional. Some blow-dry their hair forever to get it just right. Women may put on their make up for an hour or more. Some people spend forever in their closet trying to find just the right combination of clothes. Others don't give a shit. They throw anything on. That's a statement too. But, everybody projects that something that they see themselves as to the world.

Who are you? What are you? What do you project to the world? And, why do you project it to the world? Do you ever think about any of this? Or, do you simply fall into the patter of zombie acceptance—doing what you do but doing it for no conscious reason?

More importantly, is how you are seen—is how you want to be seen, who you truly are and what you truly are? Or, it is simply an illusion created in your own mind in hopes of making people believe that you are something that you truly are not?

Next time you are thirsty think about all of the water you have wasted.

Next time you are hungry remember all of the food you have wasted.

Few people desire to meditate. They do not feel that they have the time or the inclination for meditation. Some think it is some weird practice that they cannot or do not want to do. Others believe that it will allow some dark spirit to enter their metaphysical being. For all kinds of reasons, all kinds of people, do not meditate.

Certainly, meditation has long been depicted as someone sitting cross-legged on the floor. And, this is one of the primary poses taught as a tool for meditation. In hatha yoga this is a specific asana that is understood to enhance meditation. But, it is essential to understand that is not the only position that once can meditate from.

The fact is, meditation can be preformed anywhere, anytime. The only requirement is that the individual chooses to take a moment or longer and silence their mind.

Some people do not meditate because they do not want to. Some people do not meditate because they think it is stupid. Some people do not meditate because they believe that they cannot. Some people do not meditate because they are too high strung. But, let's leave all that Mind Stuff behind for moment. Right now, take a moment, close your eyes, and let go. Just be silent for a moment. This is no race. This is no endurance contest. Just take a moment, let go, and feel the silence.

If you do this, and you actually did it, you will realize in that moment of Not Trying a little bit of peace came over you. You became just a little bit calmer.

Meditation is not hard to do, though people frame it that way in their mind. In fact, it takes no effort at all; you just simply need to let go.

So, let's discuss a couple of simple meditation techniques that you can employee anywhere, any time that do not require you sitting cross-legged on the floor.

As just discussed, simply close your eyes and let go. For a moment, right now, stop your mind. Consciously breathe out all of the stress and negativity that is in your being, and be free. There is no time requirement for this meditation. Just do it for a long as you feel like doing it.

This is a very simply, very useful meditation technique. You can do this when you find yourself upset or angry. You can do this when you find yourself happy. Or, you can do it when you simply want to take a moment and step away. You can do it anytime to recenter your being and calm your mind.

Meditation does not have to be performed with your eyes closed. You're in a traffic jam and you need to be at an appointment. Without closing your eyes, simply release. Turn off the radio. Mentally remove yourself from all of the chaotic energy that is surrounding you. Consciously let go of all that angst that is reverberating in your mind and be free. Breathe out, let go of all the negativity that is being instigated by your surroundings. Let go and feel the meditative peace.

You can do this for a few seconds or you can do for a few minutes. You can do it for a long as you are in the car if you want to. It is up to you.

What actually occurs in meditation is that you take control over your mind and instead of letting the emotions of the moment control you, you control them. It is very easy all you have to do is let go.

Meditation does not have to be a formalized process where you force yourself to sit in padma asana for hours on end. It can be done in a moment, any moment, where you just want to recenter your mind and emerge with a calmer more profound perspective about your life and your place in reality.

The Ethereal Plane
and Its Material Manifestation
21/Jan/2020 10:14 AM

For anyone who has studied the occult spirituality that was written about in the later eighteen hundreds and into the early twentieth century, they will understand that the discussion about *The Ethereal Plane* was a central focus. Certainly, this concept historically dates back much farther but as publishing became affordable and became the way many people expanded their understanding of human reality this was one of the central talking points for those seeking a widow into the ultimate meaning of life and what exists in the Great Beyond. Through the writings of people like Madam Blavatsky and Dion Fortune discussions and depictions of *The Ethereal Plane* came to be embraced in the minds of many.

In essence, *The Ethereal Plane* is the otherworldly location where the spirits dwell: the guardian angels, the spirit helpers, the demons, and the spirits of those who have left their life behind. It is the vast uncharted sourcepoint of the abyss where one travels in meditation to reach the depths of human and spiritual understanding.

In this modern era, the study of, the travel to, and the embracing of *The Ethereal Plane* is left to those few remaining individuals who seek to employ the powers and the understanding posses by those of *The Great Beyond*. Today, it is far less spoken of than it was in times gone past. This, however, does not change the essence of this mystical plane.

Whether it is a real place or simply something conjured up in the mind of some mystic is almost unimportant. What is important is that, to many, it is an actual place of existence—it is real. Think about how many people seek the guidance of a psychic. Think how many séances have been performed. Where are these people traveling to gain their insight? Answer, *The Ethereal Plane.*

Therefore, as it has been so long studied, discussed, written about, and traveled to, at least in the minds of those who view this place as real, it is real. Thus, no matter how some people deny the fact of its validity, as it was and is believe to be an actual location, it has become an actual abode at least in the minds of those who believe. Though based in the mind, it is no less real than the reality we each live on a daily basis.

Through the writings and talks on or about *The Ethereal Plane* the pundits always have stated that this is the place where we, as the living and breathing, are either helped or hurt. It is from this plane that our guardian angels function as well as it is the place from where we are psychically attacked.

As we all understand, all things are born in the mind. As we all should understand, the more you think about anything the more that thing becomes a reality in your life. What you continually think about in your mind manifests into physical reality. As so many for so long have contemplated *The Ethereal Plane* has it manifested into reality? What reality you ask? Answer, the internet.

Think about it, the internet is that uncharted realm where the uncontrollable takes place. Can you control the internet? No. Can I? No. Can anyone? No.

Good things are given to us from the internet. Bad things are done to us from the internet. All these occurrences take place. Its vastness continues to expand. And, we have no control over it.

Just like *The Ethereal Plane* there are those who claim they can travel to it and embrace its knowledge. Most of us can make that claim. The internet is a bit easier to access, yet it is no less knowable or controllable than *The Ethereal Plane.* Though some may be able to control individual elements of the internet, no one has the absolute wisdom to regulate its vastness. Thus, gifts are given to us and pain is imparted onto us and we have no absolute control over either.

The life of the mind is always what pushes the boundaries of reality. The life of those who wish to expand the mind is what charts new levels of reality for all of us. The creativity and focus of the mind is what sets new life definitions into motion. It is also what causes the ethereal to melt into conscious and known reality.

With the birth of the internet *The Ethereal Plane* was provided with a physical reality. No less controllable but at least more knowable.

The internet is *The Ethereal Plane.* It has simply been provided with a new name.

*   *   *

20/Jan/2020 02:21 PM

The more you talk the more you say things that aren't worth saying.

36

Are Your Mistakes Really Mistakes?
20/Jan/2020 09:38 AM

I believe that each of us has set about doing some something and when we get to the end of it we realize that we have done it wrong. With this, we must go back and redo it. Frustrating... Especially frustrating when it is something that we really don't want to do in the first place. But, this is life and that's the way it plays out sometimes. We do something wrong. We make a mistake. We have to accept what we are left with or we have to redo it. But, is a mistake really a mistake?

I've often spoken about this in terms of filmmaking and particularly *Zen Filmmaking;* that there are no mistakes. That if you allow what you have created to be what it is, then your filmmaking process is set free. It has become True Art because you are not attempting to dominate the outcome with some preconceived notion.

So many filmmakers, so many musicians, so many artist have a specific idea in mind about how their piece is suppose to come out. They do it, they don't like it, they redo it and redo it. This may go on forever. In some cases it causes them to just trash the whole project, as it did not manifest as they had seen it in their mind. But, what is in your mind? It is the idealize outcome to the All and the Everything. It is perfection, at least as you envision it. But, how often is life ever like that?

Think about this, what if you just let things be as they are. If you do what you do, and you do your best, but it comes out differently than you had imagined. Is this new outcome any less than the one you saw in your mind or it simply just a different manifestation of creation?

Some people hold themselves to the expected—to the what is expected. Are those people free? Are they truly the artists? Or, are they simply someone who is attempting to give others what is the most commonly accepted?

If you free yourself from the concept of this is right that is wrong—this is the way it should be verse that is a mistake, think of the beauty your life will embellish. You will do and what you do will be perfect. Sure, it may not be what you saw in your mind's eye but it is free, whole, and complete onto its own suchness.

Is anything really a mistake?

The Business Model of Making Money
19/Jan/2020 08:23 AM

Virtually everyone needs a method of making money to survive. There is surviving and then there is thriving. Some people find that pathway to make a lot of money with little personal investment and from this they thrive. Others/most must work for their living. Though this is the common pattern of life, there are many levels to how a person finds a way to survive.

Think about organizations, based around thrift stores, like *The Goodwill*. Here is an interesting business model. Their entire business strategy is based around the fact that people give them stuff for free and then they sell it. That's a pretty good way to make a living don't you think?

There are other organizations that do this like *The Salvation Army*. But, they have a different internal business model and mindset. Though they make a large percentage of their money from the sales of items given to them at their thrift stores, they are a large religiously-based charitable group, founded in the 1800s, that actual has centers and living spaces set up where they provide housing and treatment for those in recovery. The same basic practice as *The Goodwill* but based around a completely different mindset.

If you are an adult, think about the people you have spoken with as you have passed through your life. What is the main focus for many of them? The answer: financial survival. Most people spend much of their lifetime working and when they are not working they are attempting to find a new/better way to make more money to survive.

In this time period, when fresh ways of gaining money via the internet have come into play, some people have charted new paths for making money and the way some people monetize their livelihood has changed. Just as in life of times gone past, there have been those who do so with a consciousness understanding of righteousness and there has been those who do what they do with little care how it affects the anyone else as long as they are making money.

Having personally watched the growth and the expansion of the internet, since its inception, I have witnessed the trends of acquisition and the rise and the fall of many people. Once upon a time, in the earlier stages, a girl could pose nude for subscribers and make a lot of money. I bumped into this one girl I knew who used to do this recently. She used to make a lot of money. Now older and with her youthful looks having faded, she lost her source of income. All that is left is angst at what to do next as she had developed no additional pathway for herself.

I have also watch, as time has progressed, and the age of internet piracy took off. People began to make money off of either stealing and offering for listening, viewing, or discussing the creations of others. The people who do that always seem to have a justification or excuses for doing what they doing. But, they are making money off of something that they had no part in creating, yet they are using that creation as a tool to make their living. Though some people who partake of this entertainment may find these free presentations appealing, there is thievery involved. What is the karma for stealing? What is the karma for receiving stolen property? And, stealing something/taking something without permission from someone is not the same as someone giving you something.

This brings us to the point of all this. What are you doing to make a living? Does how you make a living help or hurt?

For example, we can look at the business model of the thrift stores. Again, a great way to make a living. Get something for free and sell it. But, then there is the subtlety. You have *The Goodwill* who takes and sells with no greater motive. Then, you have *The Salvation Army* who takes and sells and uses that money to help people in need.

What you do to make a living defines who and what you are and what karma you will encounter later in your life. Does what you do to financially survive set the stage for a greater good or does what you do to financially survive simply serve yourself and your need for you to get what you want?

It's for you to decide what you do. But remember, whatever you do always comes with a price. A price you may not pay until tomorrow.

*   *   *

19/Jan/2020 07:31 AM

How many people are asking god for help right now?

How many people are receiving it?

Can You Help Too Much?

When I was coming up in life, Karma Yoga was the name of the game. As I was associated with Eastern Spirituality, Selfless Service was commonly taught as one of the highest pathways to personal, spiritual, and global betterment. Me, I was always happy to help.

If someone needed their house painted, help with moving, someone to run their sound system for a concert or event, a stagehand, you name it... I was happy to do it for free. I mean, I was Swami Satchidananda's soundman, traveling all around the West Coast on my own dime, using my own equipment; no charge. I was the person who collected the $2.00 entry fee for the Sufi Dances (The Dances of Universal Peace), every Tuesday night; no charge. I literally taught the marital arts for free everyday of the week for this man for nearly a decade. It was not so bad in the early days as I was working towards my BA at Cal State Northridge, which was near the studio, but after I graduated I moved to Hermosa Beach so I drove from Hermosa to Reseda everyday. Not close but, no problem! I even loaned that guy money when he needed it. Me, I never got paid or paid back—not one dime. But, I was fine with it. I was happy to help. That's Karma Yoga!

When I got into the film game, it was common that I didn't get paid in the early days. As an actor or as a member of a film crew, I was happy to help. No money, no problem. I was happy to help guide the production towards its completion.

When I was a teenager, still living with my mother, she would get so frustrated with me. *"You need to get paid,"* she would exclaim. But, it wasn't about that. It was about helping.

As the 1980s came into full swing and Yuppies and the *"Me,"* generation took hold, I watched as the mindset of people radically changed. Everybody started only thinking and caring about themselves. People still wanted and were still asking for help. People still hoped to get that help for free. But, the mindset of the generation began to change. No longer was it about helping... No longer was it, help me and I'll help you. No longer was it one person willing to help the other person just because they could. No longer was it about Selfless Service and Karma Yoga. It became about one or more people getting what they wanted. ...Getting it as freely as possible just so they could get it.

Did people really change that much? I don't know??? Or, was it simply that the people I encountered and interacted with had changed? If so, than that was my fault. If not... Well...

I had this long-term girlfriend at one point in time. Crazy relationship... My fault, I was an asshole and a horrible womanizer. But, when we finally went our separate ways when I meet this other person that really grabbed hold of me, I thought back on our years together. I even concluded one of my books commenting on it. I mean, I had paid, at least in part, for that girl to get a degree. I bought her a car. I took her on so many road trips I can't even remember the number. Free, no charge. I had flown her around Europe. I bought her furniture for her apartment. I loaned her so much money it's not even funny, always with the promise I would be paid back... But, when we went our separate ways; that was that. She never paid me a dime. I joked, (in that novel), I wish I could do that with my bills. Did I wish her any ill will? Of course not. I was happy to give when I could give. But, it did come illustrate the changing mindset of at least some people. People want. People take. Other people are willing to give. Some people don't care about what their taking will do to that other person or that other person's life. Then what?

I do not believe the concept of Karma Yoga; Selfless Service has changed one iota in the reality of reality. It is all about how people process it. Moreover, it is not like you can or should calculate who should receive help and who does not deserve it because then the only criteria becomes based upon personal appraisal. And, there is no spirituality in that.

I often hear people talking and I see it all over the internet; people discussing what they want. I hear and see people not happy about what they are being given. I also hear and see a lot of regret discussed when somebody has given somebody something but they received nothing or not what they expected in return.

Here's the thing... If you're only thinking about yourself, you are not thinking about the other person. If this is the case, if you are locked into a mindset of self-involvement, then there is no way that you can exist on the level of Karma Yoga.

Karma Yoga, Giving, and Helping is not about YOU. It is about Giving. It is about Helping. It is about hoping to make someone else's something a little bit better. No payment, no problem. No acknowledged thank you, no problem. Why? Because you did what you did for that other person. You did what you did to help them. You did what you did to make the All and the Everything just a little bit better. Therefore, you do not care about getting paid. You do not care about receiving a thank you.

Karma Yoga is about helping someone/anyone who needs help. That's it!

Help everyone you can. That's the motto. That's the mantra. Help. No payment required.

You can believe what you believe but that doesn't change what anyone else believes.

*   *   *

17/Jan/2020 08:35 AM

Most people do not want to hear the truth about their life.

Commentating is Not Experiencing

17/Jan/2020 08:32 AM

Life is live by enacting experience. Wisdom is gained by studying personal life experiences and learning from them.

For each of us we interact with life in a unique manner. We see, we experience, we process, and then we conclude defined solely by our own mind. This is the common pattern of life.

The main thing that holds anyone back from actually experiencing human evolution is, however, when the individual does not instigate the unique experience of their own life and, instead, limits their internal reflection to examining and commentating upon the experiences of others.

Studying the life of another person is very easy. Describing the life of another persons is very easy. Pontificating about the life of another person is very easy. Why? Because it takes no personal effort. It does not involve experiencing life on one's own terms. All it takes is analyzing and then liking or disliking what someone else has done.

We see this all the time in life. Some people are born with the inability to truly step outside of the themselves and their environment and to move towards the realm of experience. In many cases, they develop all kinds of excuses to hide this fact. But, as in all cases, an excuse is nothing more than an excuse.

Other people after encountering negative life experience fall into the realm of seclusion. Once one is secluded a person has one of two options. The first is to truly retreat into the meditative mind and travel to the sourcepoint of human consciousness where they can then come to understand the realities of the inner self. But, this is a difficult pathway only undertaken by a very few. More commonly the individual who falls into this reclusive lifestyle simply turn their minds outwards and focus on the life actions and the life experiences of those who are still out there doing. Though this is the common pathway of those who decide not to follow a pathway of person life experience, all it leads to is a life of debate with no personal understanding gained. Why? Because true-life understanding can only be gained via personal experience. It can never be gained solely by studying or discussing the life actions of another person.

Most of us want to live, most of us want to love, most of us wish to experience life for we understand that this is where true knowledge comes from. Some, however, find that they can cast a larger shadow by focusing on the words and the actions of others. But, what the person who follows this pathway never truly takes the time to understands is that all they have done is to shift the power of their actually coming to know the truth of their own reality to the mind of someone else. They are simply basing their existence on detailing the words and the deeds of someone else. Thus, they can never reach personal realization.

It is for this reason that it is essential that any person who is walking the path of consciousness never relay upon the analysis of the commentator. Because they do not truly understand the reality of reality. They do not truly know what they are talking about. All they have done is to follow a person who has actually accomplished something and then they cast their appraisal onto that person's actions.

50

The fact is, no one can ever truly know what is in the mind of another person. Therefore, to discuss what any person thinks or believes is taking place proves that they have no true knowledge about the reality of human existence.

In life, if you want to know there is only one way to know. That way is to live, to do, to experience. If you want to know the truth about anything do it, live it but never believe that any person who speaks about anything, who has not personally lived that something, has any true knowledge to pass along to anyone.

17/Jan/2020 08:32 AM

Isn't it a higher calling to create somethings of your own than to discuss what someone else has created?

17/Jan/2020 08:32 AM

How can you find someone from your past when you can't remember their name?

Each Day is an Interesting Day but Interesting Only Happens When You Go Outside
16/Jan/2020 12:45 PM

I was driving down the street today when up ahead I noticed there was this young man standing in the middle of the street. The guy had long hair. Shoulder length but it was trimmed. He had a straggly beard, which is quite common these days. From his appearance, he did not seem that abnormal.

He was standing right in the middle of two lanes on the street. As I and the other cars on the street approached, he would kind of shift his positioning. Not really trying to get out of the way but seemingly more to shift with the energy of the approaching cars. The one thing that was very noticeable about him, at least for those of us who have an eye for such things, is that as I drove past I could see that he had that distance in his eyes. Distance, like he was dupped up on Acid.

This all set me to thinking and to once again realizing how all life is tied together.

Early in the day I was having breakfast at one of my usual haunts. As is the case with everywhere I frequent, I become friendly with the staff. As I was leaving one of the servers told me about how her boyfriend was being stalked by this woman and how at every turn there she was.

I asked, was she a former girlfriend, but she claimed she was not. My initials thought was that the guy was probably hitting it on the side and the stalker believed his words of love and that is why she was not giving up the fight. I mean, men will be men…

But, all of that sent me to thinking about stalkers. Have you ever had a stalker? I've had a couple: off-line and on. But, a particular one comes to mind.

Now, I've told this story, (probably far better), in a piece of literature or a poem, but I was up at this art exhibit opening in San Francisco back in the 80s. There I met this girl who had that same distant look in her eyes as the guy in the street did today. I thought she was just dupped up on Acid. One thing lead to another, we left together, turned down a request from a leather-clad Swinger couple that wanted us to party with them, went and had a couple of drinks at this high end bar, and ended up back at her place. Where... Well, you know...

The next day, I wake up and realize she still had that distant look in her eyes. It wasn't Acid. It was that she was schizophrenic. Fuck me!

We spent the day together. I keep trying to leave but when I finally push the matter in the evening, she went berserk. She did not want me to leave. Now, this woman was pushing six feet tall and well put together. I really thought I was a going to have to fight my way out of her apartment. But finally, with the promises of tomorrow that each player says to his women, I was gone, hoping to never see her again.

Maybe a month or so later I come home with my girlfriend to my on the beach apartment. There were a million sticky notes all around my door. The SF girl had tracked me down. How, I do not know, but she did. Full on stalker!

My main girlfriend at the time was this feisty Glam Slam Chinese girl based out of West Hollywood. She was a take no shit kind of girl. So, when the stalker popped out of my neighbor's apartment I was concerned about what would happen next. I thought she might kick her ass.

To side bar here... My advice to all young men is to always keep a main girlfriend. That way you have all of your options in place. Then, play the field on the Low. From this, you never know what level of life perfection you may encounter. But remember, there is always a price...

My main girlfriend and I were not really what you could call monogamous, though we pretended to each other that we were. But, that is all beside the point...

The people who believe that there is a chance for something, stalk people. They want something from that other person. But, it is only they who want it. Not the person they are stalking. That person just wants to live his or her own life without the intrusion. But, a stalker is lost in the distorted reality of their own mind. They believe that by continually encountering the person of their desires, that person will give them what they want even if they don't have it to give.

For me, finally after threating to call the police the stalker girl left me alone. What will happen with my restaurant friend and her boyfriend, I do not know? But people, you gotta realize if a person doesn't want to hang out with you, (even if they have hit it and quit it), you gotta let 'em go. They will never be able to give you what you think you want from them.

But, to the point—at least one of them... Based on what my server friend had said, I was thinking about that girl with the distance in her eyes for the first time in a very long time. And then, there is he was... That guy with the same gaze, dancing in the street. All life is connected.

As I drove past, in my rearview, I saw the guy continue to dance in traffic. He got right in front of one car. The car stopped and then drove around him. Acid or schizophrenia, I do not know? I do know that both are not good. What I am sure of is that living life is so revealing if you just open up your eyes. But, you have to live life for it to be revealed.

Each day is an interesting day but interesting only happens when you go outside.

*   *   *

16/Jan/2020 08:25 AM

Most everybody tries to become somebody. Take a moment right now, consciously let go of your thoughts and watch yourself become nobody.

How free did you just become?

16/Jan/2020 07:14 AM

Take a moment right now and really appreciate all that you have.

Pairing spirituality with modern life is a tricky business. As I often discuss, most people don't care about spirituality. They care about getting over. They care about having. They care about getting what they want. But, for the few people who do care about raising their consciousness and making the world a better place it is not often an easy balance to find the perfect mix of Spirituality and Materialism.

Having grown up in a time when Eastern Spirituality was very prevalent in the minds of the masses, there was discussions and depictions of it everywhere. The promises it offered where commonly peddled to the rank and file. This is not to say that a larger number of people were actually embracing spirituality compared to today, it is simply that for those of us who did have the inclination it was far more available.

As many of you know, I spend a number of years under the guidance of Swami Satchidananda. I became close to the man, his teaching, and his institute. Well, at least as close as a disciple can be. I was his soundman. He seemed to like to me. I was following the path of brahmacharya, And, all was well with the world. My youthful plan was to go to India and live as a monk forever.

The thing about spirituality, at this point in history, was that there was an undefined blending of Eastern and Western mentality. The two of which are obviously very different. Within this, there were many Westerners, like myself, who came to be involved in the teachings. The problem was and is; Westerners are not from the East. We grew up with a completely different set of internal standards. Thus, the blending was not always coherent or easy.

For example, there was this one disciple of Swami Satchidananda who had taken the vows of celibacy. This was the first step on the formal pathway to becoming a Sannyasin. He lived at the Santa Cruz, California ashram.

During this period of time, there were a number of the people who belonged to orthodox Eastern spiritual groups, like the Integral Yoga Institute (IYI), that blended music into their practice. Aside from the traditional kirtan we used to chant, a few of the members started a band.

Certainly, having grown up in a world of Rock n' Roll, I too played music. I loved music! But, I was not a formal initiate on the pathway towards Sannyas. So, I always thought this was a little weird to have or to be in an IYI rock band when you were a monk.

One day, the proverbial shit hit the fan. This person, who was the bass player in the band, had a sit down with Gurudev and told him he wanted to be a Rock Star. Though I am certain this was always something in his mind, being allowed to be placed at the forefront of the disciples by playing music and getting admiration fueled his internal fire. We were all sitting around in a small group at the time and Swamiji could not believe it. Not to elongate this point, the guy left the order with one of the other women who was also an initiated brahmacharya. He was off to find Rock Stardom, which he never did.

Here is the thing about formalized spirituality and one of its biggest downfalls. If you are Something, you are Something. You can claim, *"I am that."* Most people have nothing to claim.

They are invisible. But, the moment you enter the Spiritual Path and you are dressed up in a uniform, (of one form or another), you instantly become something. People are looking at you. You can claim that you are some sort of a knower. Sure, this is all bullshit. But, think how many people fall into this trap. And with, *"Being spiritual,"* at the top of the list of life accomplishment for many people, for someone who is walking this path, they are fed the Rock Star Dream. They have become, *"That Something."*

Just look at Swami Satchidananda. He too was a Rock Star. He was the man who opened Woodstock. He had people flock to his lectures and he had tons of devotees.

Again, this is where the blending of the Eastern mindset of spirituality verses the Western mindset hits a bump in the road. The person from the East, the person who was born and educated in India, has a specific cultural understanding about what it means to walk the path of Sannyas. The Westerner, on the other hand, has a distorted understanding. They see it as pathway to becoming, not a pathway of egoless nothingness.

Certainly, Swami Satchidananda had his critics. I have written about this in other places. I mean, he owned a beautiful house in Montecito, California, drove a vintage Cadillac, flew a plane, had a beautiful woman (his secretary) living with him. I mean, come on… We all know what was going on. He was a Rock Star!

An interesting thing that happened in association with that woman a few years later was at this one small gathering Swamiji suggested that we each donate something to be auctioned to raise money for the L.A. IYI. *"His Secretary,"* offered up this beautiful, obviously very expensive, shawl. I was going to buy it for my girlfriend. But, out of the corner of my eye I could see Swamiji shaking his head, *"No,"* to her. As he had obviously bought it for her. The shawl was pulled back from the auction. This made me smile.

Another funny/interesting remembrance was this one incident that took place at the L.A. IYI. This one disciple, who was living there, wanted to drink coffee in the morning. The rest of the disciples had a problem with the smell, etc., being broadcast during morning meditation. We were sitting in the living room with Gurudev and the subject was brought up. He joking exclaimed that he too liked to drink coffee in the morning that's way he didn't live at the ashram. Thus, it was a no-go for the disciple's morning coffee. But, Swamiji got to drink his in house on the hill in Montecito.

This is the ideal depiction of how he lived his life. Yes, he was the teacher. Yes, he taught the path of celibacy, abstinence, and renunciation but did he live it? No, not really…

Later in time, after I had left the clique a number of women threw allegations his direction. True? Probably. But, does that even matter? Did it change his teachings? No. In life, it is all about what you make of anything. You life is your fault.

It is kind of like what happen to Swami Kriyananda of the Yogananda Order. He was a Westerner and one of the early initiates of the order. After spending much of life as a monk and eventually setting up his own ashram, he met a woman, left celibacy behind, and married her. Eventually, it all got very messy, as divorces tend to do. I mean, my sister-in-law is paying her ex a ton of palimony each month. I just think that's wrong; a man should be a man. But anyway... It eventually played out, the woman got paid, and Kriyananda dropped the Swami from his name. Who's to blame? A man for being a man and a woman for being a woman? Or, the fact that Kriyananda was basing his existence upon a spiritual platform and then fell in love? Again, this is the problem with finding a balance between life and spirituality...

Spirituality is a complicated process. It is especially problematical when traditions are blended and formalized rituals are left behind.

Me, I have based my entire existence upon blending the traditional with the nonbinding. But, I don't claim to do anything else. Do I sell people promises to embrace spirituality? No, I give them away. Do I lie about who I am and what I do? No, I do not.

This is the whole thing... In essence we are all the same. We want what we want. Some of us simply wish to place the focus on the Realm of Spirituality—by whatever name you call it. Some of us what to make the world a better place and to help people become just a little bit happier. But, to do that you need to remove your ego from the equation. You cannot only be thinking about yourself, the titles you hold, and what you want. You have to think about the needs of the Greater Whole.

Try it. Let go. Believe me you will feel a thousand times more free.

Think about helping people instead of only thinking about yourself and again, believe me, the everything of your everything will become a million times better.

Being spiritual does not mean that you will now hold the title of, *"Spiritual."* Being spiritual does not mean that because you are spiritual you are now a, *"Something."* In fact, it should be just the opposite. What you are should be kept hidden. Let your actions of goodness speak for themselves. From this, your ego will be kept in check and you can never be accused of using the, *"What you are,"* as anything but a means to make everybody's everything just a little bit better.

Virtually everyone seeks adventure in their life. They seek to live an exciting, rewarding, adventurous existence. They seek to develop memories that they can proudly tell to others. The problem is, there is always a price for adventure.

Everywhere you look there are advertisements for travel. They each promise a joyous time. What is the cost of that time?

You see car ads on a daily basis. Many times they depict the driver encountering some great experience somewhere after having gotten to that experience in the car. Real or fantasy and what is the unseen cost?

There are advertisements for bicycles and motorcycles. Have you ever been in a bike wreck or a motorcycle accident? The price is very high.

The thing about adventure is that it is the promised illusion. It is what you don't know compared to what you believe it will be. But, what is never seen, at least before the fact, is the price that will be paid for the experience that is had and the fact that once anything is lived it is realized that it was never what was expected. How could it be?

Many people write and speak of their own encountering(s) of adventures. I too have done that. If you want to know the real me, read my novels and my poetry for those are made up of the experiences I have lived on the most emotional level. Like I have long said, my autobiography has already been written. But, no matter what I or anyone else writes, those are my adventure they are not your adventures. My adventures can never be your adventures, just as your adventures can never be mine.

People believe that the *Out There* promises so much more than the *In Here*. That illusion is one of the driving factors of life and that is the illusion that the salesmen draw upon to send you down a passageway to the dreams they promise. But, it is they who are selling and you who are buying. They are getting paid and you are spending. Who is doing what and why? Do you ever question this as you walk towards the promise of adventure?

Some people, including myself, always try to explain that one should make the mundane an experience in and of itself. That one should look at the everyday and see the newness in every action, no matter how many times those actions were done. This is a tool. This is a meditation. But, this too is a means to keep the mind focused on the outside, not the inside.

Think about a time you did something and afterwards you felt that you had spent way too much money doing it. Think about a time you did something that you thought was going to be a great and big adventure and it turned out to be far less of an ideal experience than you had hoped. Maybe it even turned into a bad experience. Was that doing worth the doing? Wouldn't it have just been better to have stayed at home?

Seeking adventure in life is a choice. No matter how much people tell you the Out There is better than the In Here, it is you who makes the choice to step outside or stay inside. Accepting the perfection of the In Here is also a choice. The main thing everyone must always keep in mind is that without falling into the arms of the seeking of adventure there is no unseen price that will be paid.

Adventure may be fun. The promise of adventure may hold appealing illusion. But, what is not known and can never be known is just what that anything will actually cost. You cannot calculate that price until it has been paid. Adventure is never free.

14/Jan/2020 07:04 AM

When do you speak to god?

Why do you speak to god?

14/Jan/2020 07:03 AM

Do you control your thoughts or do you thoughts control you?

*   *   *

How often do you become upset by something that does not affect you directly?

How Can I Help You?
13/Jan/2020 07:29 AM

I was watching TV last night and on this show this one character said to another, *"How can I help you?"* This was a very genuine question. The character really wanted to provide some help to the other man. The set me to thinking... I realized that no one has ever asked me that question. This is not to say that certain people have not helped me throughout my years but no one ever questioned what is the one thing that I really needed help with at a specific point in time.

The thing about people helping and about the human nature of most people in general is that, people generally want a return for what they do. They are willing to help someone else only when it benefits them in some manner. Whether this so-called, *"Help,"* is going to lead them towards career advancement, lifestyle placement, money, sex, fame, someone to go to the movies with, or whatever, people generally want something in return for any help they provide.

This common mindset and ideology long ago led me to the semi-joking conclusion about my life, *"Everybody wants something from me but nobody ever gives me anything."*

Think about your own life... Who has directly asked you, *"How can I help you?"* Once asked, did they follow through and actually provide you with the help you needed?

Think about your own life... Who have you directly asked, *"How can I help you?"* Once answered, did you follow through and actually provide them with the help they needed? Or, did you never even think to ask this question?

Moreover, do the people you association with ever even think of asking this question or do they only think about themselves, their own wellbeing, and what they do or do not want? Do you ever even think of asking this question or do you only think about yourself, your own wellbeing, and what you do or do not want?

In life, I believe we all hope for help when we need it. In life, I believe we all eventually realize that help is not readily available. Though most of us probably wish that this were different, it is not.

So, what can we do with information? Probably the only viable option is for it to be an inspiration for us to personally change—for us to be the one wiling to provide help. ...For us to be the one who asks, *"How can I help you?"* And, once the question is answered to set about on a course to actually do what we can to make the life of that other person just a little bit more, *"Helped."*

Do You Believe in Jesus?

11/Jan/2020 07:47 AM

"Scott, Do you believe in Jesus?"

I bumped into a guy that was in a fairly successful band during the New Wave/Punk days. …Successful at least here in L.A. They had a hit song or two and I would see them playing the L.A. club scene all the time.

It was actually a great time in L.A. In the 1970s through the 1980s L.A. had a great club scene.

At some point the guy had left all that behind and now makes his way as a troubadour playing acoustic guitar in small clubs. …Though I don't know how he makes a living at that, as those places really don't pay much nor do indie record labels. Maybe he has a wife with a nine-to-five or something. I don't know?

Anyway, it had been decades since I had spoken with him but pretty much the first words out of his mouth were that question, *"Scott, Do you believe in Jesus?"* Me being who I am, of course, all that set me to thinking…

I always find people who are very outwardly Christian a very interesting breed. They wear their religion on their sleeve and base all of their reality upon it. I mean when I have met Christian girls who find me attractive you can always see they are trying to size me up and see if I would fit into their boyfriend mold by waiting for my response to them after they intentionally say something about the lord being with them and stuff like that.

You know, what a person believes in is all-good with me. If that's what makes you who you are, rock on! Me, however, I have my own thoughts about religion…

Being born into a Christian family I, of course, was sent to Sunday school and church at least for a small part of my childhood. I was programmed into the fact that I needed to say my prayers, ask for forgiveness for my sins, and recite the Lord's Prayer every night before I went to sleep; which I did quite diligently. But, a turning point happened when my dog died of Korean Distemper.

I was a latch key kid, long before that term was invented. I was also an only child. Somehow my parents thought it was okay to leave a five, six, seven year old kid home alone all day when they were at work. I had my shows to watch. I did yoga and meditation with Richard Hittleman who was then on the UHF channel twenty-eight here in L.A. But mostly, I had my dog.

Previously to that, I had a dog when I was very young. I'm one of those people who can remember back very early into my childhood and when I was like two I had the croup, was locked in my crib, and the dog came to visit me. I think he loved me, as he was a furry black and white guy whose tale was always waging when he was around me. When I got better I asked about my dog. My mother's answer was that he had caught the croup from me and he died. Throughout my life that thought haunted me, that I had killed my dog. It wasn't until I was in my late-thirties and talking to my shrink one day that I had the realization that, *"Dog's don't get the croup!"* My mother had lied! She just didn't want the dog anymore and gave me that as an excuse as to why it was gone. How fucked up is that? And, that just lets you know the kind of bad, psychologically damaging parenting I lived through.

But, a few years pasted, I was out with my father one day, we stopped by a pet shop and on the spur of the moment he bought me a dog. I loved that dog. He and I spend all our days together. But, he got sick after a year or so and died. I was devastated. I prayed every night for god to bring me another dog. To this day, nothing... Though my friend and I did go up to San Francisco in the early 1970s and this hippie girl was giving away puppies in Haight Ashbury and I got one and brought it home to the apartment I lived in. The next day I went to high school. I come home and my mother had given it away but she would not tell me to whom. Not good! I was very sad.

But, all of this brings the discourse to the concept of Jesus and god. Many Christians visualize god in the form of Jesus. I mean, go to the Church of the Holy Sepulcher in Jerusalem and you will see people going emotionally nuts.

Me, as a child, I always envisioned god more as an omnipresent void in the vast out-thereness. But, I would pray and pray for a new dog and still nothing...

Christians always tell people that god has a plan, that god is testing you, and all that kind of stuff. Me, I just think that is all denial, justification, and bullshit being mouthed by a person who wants to find rationalization and confirmation where there is none.

I am no biblical scholar but I have read and studied the bible and the books that did not make it into the bible. I have consumed a lot of information about the history of Christianity and its evolution so I have at least a somewhat substantial knowledge about the religion beyond its most elemental level of faith. But, isn't that all religion is? Faith. Believing to believe. Believing to have something to believe in. Believing so that you can assess a reason to your life; your trials, your tribulations, and your joys? And, the promise of forever in heaven if you are good. What is heaven?

I mean, most of the world believes in god in one form or the other. It seems that people need a reason to believe. And, people need a focus for that belief. For some, that focus is Jesus.

Now, there are historians who question whether Jesus ever physically existed or not. Maybe he did, maybe he didn't? But, that is almost not even the point. Whether he lived as a man or not, think about all of the things that have happened based in the name of Jesus; both good and bad. Think about all of the people who believe in and pray to Jesus everyday. Is there a day that goes by where you don't hear or see something about Jesus? Whether you believe in him, worship him or the concept of Jesus or not, the fact is, Jesus is one the major defining factor of world history.

"Scott, Do you believe in Jesus?"
"Yes, I do."

We Are All Dominated By the Actions of Others
10/Jan/2020 10:49 AM

We are all dominated by the actions of others. Look at your life. Think about the things that have happened to you both good and bad. Though you may have been the one who instigated the doing of any action it was someone else who altered and ultimately defined the outcome.

Each person's life is defined by where they live and when they live. Like I have long said, just think about the fact that if you had done something just one minute later from when you did what you did then the outcome may have been totally different. ...If you left home one minute later that person would not have run into your car. If you had left your office one minute earlier that person would not have bumped into you as you were walking down the street and attempted to start a fight with you. If you had not gone out on the town when you did you would not have met that person and fallen in love. The list goes on but all of life activities (both positive and negative) are defined by the actions of others.

The defining actions of others span the gambit from the very small to the very large. But, it is that someone else that creates those moments. Maybe a person smiles at you and makes your life just a little bit happier as you are passing by one another. Maybe somebody does some dastardly deed that really messes with your life and your livelihood. You were you but it was them who chose to do that something and from that action your life was altered.

I think back to an example that happened in my life. On a whim I had bought this Porsche 914. I was driving around with the top off and my then girlfriend riding shotgun when I got a flat tire. I had the car jacked up and was attempting to change the tire but the lug bolts had been put on with an air gun and I had not yet learned the secret to pop them with anything less than brut force. I mean, I was still relativity young and I was a skinny guy. I weight like a buck fifty. I was standing there trying to figure out what to do next when this big burly bearded guy pulls up in his junky pickup truck, gets out, comes over a bam the lug nut was freed. *"I work at an auto shop I do this stuff all day,"* he exclaimed. *"Thanks!"* He didn't have to do that but he saw a situation where he could help and he did help. How often do you do that? How often does anyone you know do that?

Here lies one of the realities of reality. What you do changes the future of other people.

Sure, there are those situations that (probably) nobody planned for like an auto accident. Sure, there are those moments when you accidentally bump into someone. Though each of those situations can set a pathway for changing a person's life into motion it is all your reaction to the action that defines the impact that you have on the life of others.

You too are the person who alters the life of other people. You too have the power to hurt, just as you too have the power to help in the next evolution of the person's life you have unexpectedly encountered. As all of our lives are dominated by what other people do to us, other people's lives are dominated by what you do to them.

What are you going to do next? What are you going to do when you encounter that next chance encounter?

The worst thing that anyone can do is to hurt someone or hurt this Life Space, never apologize, and never attempt to fix the wrong they have committed.

The best thing that anyone can do is to help someone or help this Life Space and ask nothing in return.

All life is based upon interaction. That interaction may be person-to-person or that interaction may be what one does to their environment.

What one does becomes the definition of their life. What one does not do also becomes the definition of their life.

As life is based upon interaction, everything someone does affects the everyone else. Even though what one person does may only have a direct effect on one other person, that person and how they are affected by what that other person has done then goes forward in life interacting with other people and the world around them based upon that interaction. Therefore, what one person does to one other person moves out, expands, and through ongoing interaction comes to affect the entire world and all of its people.

What you do, good or bad, to one person may seem like a very small thing to you but what you do has affected that other person and, as such, will cause them to react and interact with other people and their life in general based upon the emotions you have created within them.

Some individuals use this formula as a means to intentionally control the mind of one or more people. They understand that by creating a happening in the life of one person that person will take the feeling and move it forward guiding people back to its source.

This is also the case with people who knowing hurt people. They understand that by creating a traumatic event in a person's life that they will then maintain a hold on the thoughts and the emotions of that person throughout their life.

On the other hand, there are some people who do very good things—very personally positive and uplifting things to and for other people. Think of someone who has said or done something nice or really helpful to you. What is your emotional response to that person? When you think of them you remember what a good, nice, and caring individual they were.

Caring should be the norm of life. Helping should be the foundational essence of any human being. We all know good when we see it, just as we all know bad. Though their may be some people who seek to call good bad and bad good based upon their own personal aspiration for a desired outcome, all anyone has to do is to look to what the doing of that something has created in someone/anyone's life and the true definition of that action becomes very clear.

The worst thing that anyone can do is to hurt someone or hurt this Life Space, never apologize, and never attempt to fix the wrong they have committed.

The best thing that anyone can do is to help someone or help this Life Space and ask nothing in return.

What are you going to base your life upon?

Most People Make Excuses
08/Jan/2020 09:39 AM

Most people make excuses for their behavior. Whether it is what they are doing to themselves or what they are doing to others, few people truly own their actions.

Many people believe they have the right to do what they want to do. They believe the have the right to consume what they wish to consume. They believe they have the right to say what they want to say about other people, no matter the consequence to the other person's life. In some cases, with some people, they believe they have the right to do what they want to do to other people. But, ask these people why they do what they do and all you will hear is a long list of excuses.

There are many excuses given for the bad actions that people commit. Most people do not even conjure up these excuses until they are questioned. They never even ponder the consequences of what they are doing, they are just doing, so they do not come up with a reason for having done what they have done until they are forced to do so.

Common excuses are, I live in a free country, I have the freedom of speech, I had a bad childhood, I am from a family of alcoholics, I was abused as a child, my friends convinced me to do it, I was hurt so I believe I should hurt others, it says so in the bible, I didn't believe that eating that food or smoking those cigarettes would actually hurt me, or I am in a psychological crisis. Of course the list goes on but at the core of what many people do is based upon the perspective of not acknowledging the fact that actions have consequences

Consequences not only to other people but also to one's self.

Think about some of the things that you have done. Why did you do them?

Think about some of the things that you are currently doing. Why are you doing them?

Think about some of the things that you have done that have affected other people in a negative manner. What was your motivation for doing them?

Go back to the moment when you did that something that had a negative effect, large or small, on your life and/or the life of someone else. Were you actually performing that action consciously or did you simply allow the action to take place with no forethought? If it was performed consciously, did you plan for the wide spanning implication that action would have on yourself and on other people or was it an action simply designed to fulfill one of your desires of the moment? If, on the other hand, you simply allowed that something to happen, why did you let it happen?

From this exercise what most people will realize is that they only think about the things that they have done in terms of an afterthought. Yes, they may have set about on a course to do something but once it is done is the only time when they realize that they must present a logical reason for doing what they have done. Thus, they create an excuse.

For some people, they create very logical excuses. They make the reason for having done what they have done seem very reasonable. But, is a coherent excuse any less of an excuse just because it sounds good?

All actions in everyone's life have consequences. Most people never even ponder this truth or question how what they are about to do is going to later affect them or impact the life of someone else. This is one of the sad truths about humanity. Most people are so locked into their own mind they never step beyond the boundaries of their own mind and when they are forced to do so at best all they can come up with is an excuse for having done what they have done.

How about you? How do you rationalize what you have previously done? How do you currently explain what you are doing? How are you justifying what you are about to do? And, are any of these definitions based upon the truth or are they only an excuse?

The Interpretation of Who You Think You Are
07//Jan/2020 07:52 AM

Who are you? How do you see yourself? How do you project yourself to the world?

How does everyone else see you? Do they see the person that you are or do they see the projection of what you hope that they will think that you are?

Are you a true person? Are you who you truly are? Do you say what you truly think or do you temper what you say, based upon how you feel, defined by the people who are around you?

Can you be true to all people or are there only a few people that know who you truly are and how you truly feel?

How many people know the truth about your life? Does any one?

Do you lie? Do you lie about who you are, what you are, what you can or cannot do, and what you have or have not achieved? Do you lie to yourself?

Do you believe that you are something when you have no proof to verify your claim? Do you tell people that you are something when you have no proof to verify your claim?

Is what you say you are, what you truly are, or is it simply a projection of your own mind?

Who knows the truth about you?

07/Jan/2020 07:52 AM

How many people's lives have you hurt to get you to where you find yourself in your life today?

Take a few moments and really think this through.

Write down a list if you wish.

What have you done to them and why?

Don't simply dismiss this exercise and don't do the, they did this to me so I did that to them or justify your actions by claiming, I've helped more people than I have hurt. Be honest with yourself, who have you hurt?

Once this person or these people are clearly defined in your mind, ask yourself this question, what am I going to do about it?

The Time That No Longer Ticks
06/Jan/2020 06:10 PM

When I was twelve I had gone over to my local Thrifty's to purchase a watch. For those of you who may not know, Thrifty's was the local chain drug store here in L.A. They were kind of the early mini-predecessor to stores like Kmart and Wal-Mart as they had a little bit of everything. They even sold electric guitars which I was saving my money up to buy but then I went on a date to Santa Monica with this girl and she spend all my savings at the penny arcade on the pier. I leaned then to never go out with rich girls because they never consider the fact that not everyone has an endless supply of money. But, that's an entirely different story...

Anyway, I saw a watch I really liked. I bought it. The thing that I thought was so cool about that watch was that it had an alarm. It was just your standard style watch but it had an extra hand and you could set it at a time and an alarm would go off. I was so happy with that watch. Just one of those simple things that really seems to make your life so much better.

Now, this was not an expensive watch. I was a kid, okay... I didn't have a lot of money. But, it was one of those things that I hoped to hold onto for a long while. But, as fate and/or cheap craftsmanship would have it, the watched died a few days later. I was really bummed, as that was the only one of that style watch that they had, so I couldn't exchange it or anything. There was nothing I could do, it was gone.

At the point I realized that winding it would no longer do any good, I sat there staring at the watch wondering/questioning, if a watch can stop calculating time did this mean that someone could stop/freeze time? If time was no longer being analyzed, did that tell me that time could be controlled? If a watch can stop, can time be stopped?

* * *

05/Jan/2020 07:35 AM

Just because you say it was a mistake doesn't mean
that you didn't do it.

*　　*　　*

02/Jan/2020 08:48 AM

Your yesterday does not have to be your today.

What Did You Expect?
02/Jan/2020 08:39 AM

Since the dawning of the #metoo movement accusations have been flying left and right. Like I've stated in the past, I too can claim #metoo. But, that's not the point... I've spoken about this in this blog, every now and then, over the past couple of years and detailed how this whole mindset is a great way for someone to take revenge on someone they are pissed off at (for one reason or another). Some of the early voices of this movement have since been shown to be not so honorable themselves. Okay... But, the ultimate question has to be asked, *"What did you expect?"*

There always seems to be some uproar when some rich, famous, or powerful person has an affair with the nanny. What did you expect? People get all up in arms when some sports star is caught cheating on his wife or girlfriend with some hot model. What did you expect? Recently, the British Royal Family was hit with one of their own allegedly hooking up with some pretty teenage girl several years back. What did you expect?

In these recent years there has been a new emphasis placed upon upstanding behavior. But, let's face facts, since the dawning of time people have been attracted to those they find attractive. And, as long as what takes place is consensual, what's wrong with that? Certainly, the mentality and mindset of the 1960s embodied a lowering of sexual morality and a freedom of sexual self-expression. Was that right or wrong? Only the people who partook have the answer to that question. Sure, there were those religious zealots who said all sex is wrong. But, on the grand scale, it was not condemned during that era. Now, times have shifted. Morality has swept society but what is the cause of that? And, is it truly focused on all-people become more whole and holy or is it simply based on a projection of judgmental morality?

It seems that at the essence of much of this time of accusations is a certain embracing of schadenfreude—a certain new way to find joy in casting blame onto someone for simply acting out what is natural. But, what is the basis of that? In fact, what is the basic of any schadenfreude? The answer, it is dissatisfaction with Self and the reality an individual is personally living.

Think about the people who cast no judgment. Who are they? What are they? They are people who are very self-confident in whatever reality they are living. Think about the people who do casting judgment and throw accusations. Who are they? What are they? They are the person who, from whatever causation factor, is insecure and dissatisfied with their life and hopes to build their self-image, in their own mind and the mind of others, by using criticism and condemnation as a tool.

But, does what some person says change reality in any way? Yes, the morals of an era are affected by the calling out of the masses but does anything on the inner reality of humanity actual change? Do you change? Do your inner desires change? Does the people you find attractive change? Does the dreams and the fantasizes about what you and that person you find attractive will do change? Probably not.

People can be programmed into a mindset of belief. Look at the world, there are so many people believing so many things. Some accept that their belief is just their belief and they let it go at that. Others attempt to force their belief into the mind of others. But, when one travels to the essence of reality, life is based upon desire. Life is given birth to by desire. You have it. I have it. What we each desire may be different but it is nonetheless essential to the foundations of all life.

So, the next time you hear about someone hooking up with some hot someone, instead of being surprised, instead of exclaiming how horrible that individual is, simply give into the truth and state, *"What did you expect?"*

The Pope Smacked Her Hand
01/Jan/2020 01:26 PM

It was kind of interesting/amusing… I was watching the news last night. The Pope, (Pope Francis), was greeting people on New Year's Eve when a devotee grabbed his hand and he angrily turned and smacked the hand of the woman who had grabbed him. As the New York Times reported it, *"In an incident captured on video and spread across the internet, Francis can be seen reaching into the crowd and seeking the hands of children. As he turns away, a woman in the crowd grabs his right hand with both of her hands and yanks the 83-year-old pope back, causing him to momentarily lose his balance. Francis, visibly upset, slaps twice at the woman's hands to free himself, rebuking her, and then angrily turns away."*

There is so many ways one can dissect this incident but no matter how you slice it, the action, equaling the reaction, details a lot about the human understanding of worship.

First of all, The Pope behaves like he is a Rock Star. And, he is… A religious Rock Star. Look at the way he presents himself to the world. He is clothed in the finest ornamented costume. He is sheltered, protected, and removed from the masses. Yet, he goes out to be revered by the masses. His counsel is sough after and he is the one who sets the tone for the entire Catholic Church. He is placed (literally) on a pedestal and a throne. He travels in bulletproof automobiles and is surrounded by bodyguards. Moreover, he knows this is the way he is viewed and he plays into. Though there is really nothing wrong with this, but don't you want a person who is considered the *Pontifex Maximus* to

94

be more than just your average ego driven personage who gets pissed off when somebody grabs them?

Think of the way famous people are treated all the time. …Famous people who are not considered holy… Think of what would have happened if they had smacked someone who had grabbed them. They probably would be sued and the person they smacked would have been interviewed on CNN.

If you don't want to be touched by people don't put yourself in a position where people can touch you.

Certainly, the role of The Pope has evolved over the years—how he is viewed and how he behaves in relation to the masses. But, to the faithful he is an icon of Christianity. Shouldn't The Pope be more than someone who gets angry and reacts without forethought?

From a person perspective, I have meet people that were considered holy men throughout my years. There were some who were truly humble and retreated from the world. There were others who played the *Holy Man Game,* took on disciples, allowed people to worship them, and embraced the power of their position. Though those are the ones who became the most well known and revered, were they truly the most holy examples of humanity?

If you are going to play a role, you really need to embrace the essence of that role. If that role claims that you are religious, holy, and/or some sort of knower, than you really need to personify that character. If you are called holy, if you are claiming to be holy, if you accept the job of being holy, than you really need to live an exemplarity lifestyle no matter what. You need to be someone and something more than someone who simply gets pissed when someone does something you don't like.

Imagine that someone is watching and listening to everything that you do. Let that be the defining factor for your behavior.

I don't think that there is any one among us who has not imagined how a situation was going to be but when that setting was actually lived it turned out totally different than we had planned.

In our Mind's Eye we had seen the situation unfold. We had planned what we would say and what we would do—what would be said to us, and how the moment would be lived. But, when it came to pass, some or none of that moment played out as we had envisioned.

For some, they plan for days what they will say and do and anticipate what others will say and do to them and for them. Of course, in the Mind's Eye one leaves room for a few variables but in some cases a person is absolutely sure how what will happen will happen. That is until it does not.

In life, a situation not playing out the way a person has hoped and people not behaving in the way a person had hoped is one of the key ingredients to disappointment. Disappointment leads to depression. It also lead to a person acting inappropriately and saying and doing things that are not very nice. Some people do not possess the ability to accept the reality of reality and from this they enact inappropriate responses.

Why do people plan out hoped for situational outcomes? Because they want to feel a certain kind of way. They want a certain something. And, the only reason they are traveling into that scenario in the first place is that they want to receive that something.

Have you ever had a Christmas morning where you did not get the gift you had hoped for?

How did you react? More importantly, how did not receiving that gift make you feel inside?

Did you ever hope a certain person would feel a certain kind of way about you? When they did not, how did that make you feel? How did that make you react?

Did you ever do something hoping to achieve something but what turned out was totally not what you hoped for? What played out was not as you had seen it in your mind. What did you do next?

The first action in your reaction is the key to who you are as a person. The way you think, equally what you hope to actualize is the definition of what you want. But, how you react to life when things do not turn out the way that you want them to is the ultimate definition of who you are.

Some people become sullen when a situation does not turn out the way they had hoped in their Mind's Eye. Some people become sad. Some people become angry and say or do negative hurtful things based upon not getting what they want. Who are you and what do you do?

As a person progress though life (at least most people) they learn to control their desire for a desired out come. Through life experience they learn that things are often not going to turn out exactly the way they want them to. From this, there emerges a tempering of the actions and reactions to life events. But, think about this, what if you didn't care? What if you had no preconceived notions about the anything of the next thing? Wouldn't that make your everything substantially more free? Wouldn't your everything become so much pure, right, and in the moment?

If you let go of visualizing what you hope for your next moment will be free. If you stop attempting to orchestrate that moment before it happens, then all things become free, you become free, and you will never be tormented by the what never was.

*   *   *

01/Jan/2020 07:25 AM

Wondering is different from worrying.

* * *

The person who tells jokes is always going to make enemies.

01/Jan/2020 07:24 AM

If you didn't know the date would you care what day it was?

*　　*　　*

31/Dec/2019 07:26 AM

Is meditation doing something or is meditation doing nothing?

You Are Not the Only Person Who Matters
30/Dec/2019 09:32 AM

Many people operate from the very selfish perspective of, Me. They think what they think, they feel what they feel, they do what they do and they never take the other person/any other person into consideration. This mindset is based upon a multitude of psychological motives but the fact of the matter is, it all boils down to one primary factor, a person does not care about what anyone else is feeling.

You can see this type of behavior all the time. When people speak negatively about other people. When people critique and criticize other people. When people steal from other people. When people hurt other people. When people make jokes about other people. And, the list goes one... But, think to a person who is behaving in the manner, who are they thinking about? Or, perhaps better put, whom are they not thinking about? The answer is, they are only thinking about themselves.

Here is the truth, whenever a person only thinks about himself or herself they exhibit behaviors that hurt other people but they do not care. They do not stop themselves. They do not stop others from being motivated by what they have instigated. Thus, a world of hurt, to the life of another person or the life of other people, is given birth to. But who care? Not the person who has instigated the hurt. Only the person who is being hurt.

If you ask the average person do they do things that hurt the life of someone else they will most likely answer, *"No."* But, is this the truth or is it simply them not being aware of the damage they are creating?

Yes, some people set about on a path of intentionally hurting other people but many do so from a mind space of oblivion. They do not realize what they are doing and, thus, they do not care. But, is the damage they are creating, by operating from unconscious mindset, any less damaging?

People are hurt by various things. What may not hurt one person will hurt another. To understand this all you have to do is to look to your own life in comparison to those you know. You are a unique individual defined by the many factors that has brought you to this point in your life. Though those you know may have had similar experiences, the way each person processes life events is entirely unique. For example, some people like to make jokes. Some people like to poke fun at others with their jokes. You may say something to one person and they may see the humor in it, say it to another person, maybe even a brother or a sister of the one person who found it amusing, and they will take offense at it. Who is the culprit? The person who likes or dislikes the joke or you for telling it? The answer is obvious.

If you don't take the time to care about how other people are feeling about what you are saying or what you are doing you are operating from a very selfish state of mind. If you don't take the time to learn from your behavior and correct the things you say and do you are operating from a space of non-caring about anyone else. If you exist from this space of unconsciousness all you leave in your wake is people that have been hurt by your words and your actions. Though some may love what you do, if you hurt anyone in doing what you do that becomes the definition of your life.

It is essential to remember the ultimate truth of life is, you are not the only person who matters.

Think before you do. Think before you speak. Think about the other person first. Then, the world becomes that much more pain-free.

*   *   *

29/Dec/2019 02:25 PM

How much time do you spend exploring?

Have you ever been sitting in a restaurant or something and there is a person sitting close to you, talking very loudly, telling some story about something and due to their volume and their proximity you are forced to listen but you can tell that what they saying is total bullshit?

Some people love to hear themselves talk. Liars always seem to be loud. They somehow believe that they have something worth saying and lost, deep somewhere within their own mind, they believe that if they are saying something to someone and that someone believes what they are saying then perhaps it becomes true. But, it is not.

People lie for all kinds of reasons. The problem with lying is that it becomes a habit/an addiction.

Some people believe a person when they lie.

Here lies the problem.

If a person who lies is believed then, at least in the mind of the believer, what the talker has spoken has become a reality.

A person believes them. Maybe they spread that lie to someone else and from this a world of belief is erected based upon nothing more that a lie envisioned in the mind of the liar.

Do you believe everything that you hear spoken from the mouth and created in the mind of someone else? Do you believe everything you hear simply because it was spoken? If you do you should perhaps rethinking your approach to belief. Because not everything spoken is based upon fact or the truth.

The Compliment You Never Give
28/Dec/2019 01:19 PM

I was having breakfast at this restaurant I have eaten at for years-upon-years. I ordered a breakfast that I have had so many times that I cannot even guess how many times I have eaten it. It arrived. I begin to eat and I realized that it was really-really good. The same eggs, the same potatoes, the same bacon, the same fruit but whatever that chef had done he (or she) really did a great job in its preparation.

I realized that though it was right there at the top of all the times that I have eaten that breakfast, there was no easy way I could tell the chef just what a great job he had done and that I really appreciated the effort he put in and how much I enjoyed the food.

It really got me to thinking about the fact that every now and then somebody really takes the time to do something right. This does not just have to do with the preparation of food but with everything. Every now and then someday really does something right but oftentimes, in those situations, you (or I) have no real method to pay them a compliment. Sad but true as I believe that all of us like to hear when someone believes that we have done something right and/or that someone appreciates what we are doing or what we have done.

I think the new exercise that should be put into practice is that whenever we believe someone has done something right that you tell them. Make the effort! Whether it is something large or it something small, reach out, make the effort and just

110

let them know that you appreciate what they are doing or what they have done.

Don't you think that would make the life of any person who does the doing just a little bit better?

When someone decided to enter the life of a monk they understand that one of the primary tenets that they will embrace is surrender. They are consciously choosing to let go of all things material in order that they may come into a more refined state of mind in order to gain a clearer communion with the divine.

The people who hope to follow this pathway are few and far between. In fact, most people do not wish, nor are they willing to live a life not defined by what they have gained.

Think to your own life. What do you think about? Do you think about having, getting, and receiving or do you think about embracing nothingness? For most, the answer is very clear. Most people want.

But, if you turn this around just a little bit, think how free your life would be if you did not have to strive to get. Think how free your life would be if you did to have to maintain what you already own.

Think about the last time you wanted a new car, how you had to strive to get the money to buy it. Think about the last time your car broke down and all the money you had to have to fix it. Think about all the energy you put into getting that woman or that man to be part of your life. Think about all the trials and the tribulations that you have encountered since they have entered your life and all of the things you have had to do and the money you have had to spend to keep them content and in your life. These are obviously just a couple of examples but wanting and getting always costs something. It is never free. And, when something is not free then an entire spectrum of karma, both positive and negative, is set into motion.

When we look across the world we see people's lives devastated when earthquakes, tsunamis, fires, tornados, or hurricanes rob people of all they have worked for. When we listen to people we hear stories of how people's lives were destroyed by overspreading, equally bankruptcy, and financial devastation. When people speak of those who they once loved but have left them, not only are they emotionally destroyed but in many cases they are financially hurt, as well.

What is the basis of all of this? The answer, desire of acquisition.

But, what if you could let go of all of this. What if you could let go of all of the things that you think you want but when you get them they were never quite what you thought they would be or they cost you an inordinate amount of something to keep them.

Many people fall into a pattern of life. They fall into a predetermined life by what they witness their family and their friends doing. They embrace a life pattern by what they believe they are expected to do. But, what comes from this? In many cases all that is born is a life defined by continued wanting, not having, or having and then losing.

But, life doesn't have to be that way. Think if you could just let go. Think if you could simply surrender.

Many people will claim that it is too late for them to embrace a life of mindful renunciation. Many will say that they have too much responsible to let go and be free. Other will say that they desire too much to ever be able to follow a pathway of conscious retreat. That may be the case but what is also the case is that you have a choice about the choices you make. Sure, you may want to live in a nice house. Sure, you may want to have a family. But, it is ultimately how you embrace those desires (or any desires) that sets the standard for your life and the state of mind you encounter as you pass through your life.

You can do things the way you were trained to do them. You can do things the way you have always done them. You can do what you believe you are expected to do but you have the option to take control and do them from a space of refined understanding about what things mean to you, what having that thing will ultimately cost you, and how by embracing a mindset of refined simplicity that you will not be dominated by external, undefined, uncalculated desires and from this come to a space of knowing that the things that you want, the things that you have do not have to be the ultimate definition of your life.

If you can take a moment for a mental meditation; let go. See the things that are causing you grief in life. View the people that are bringing disharmony to your life. Witness the things that you always do that are doing bad things to you, your life, and the life of those you know. Now, mentally let go. Let go of all of those things. Surrender. See your life without them. What is it like? You can live your life that way if you desire to do so.

Your life can be lived any way you choose to live it. You can do good things from a space of positivity or you can do bad things. You can desire, you can seek your desire(s), you can obtain your desire(s). But, what is the cost? What is the cost to

114

you, your inner peace, your pathway to realization, and to others?

Imagine if you let it all go. How free you would be. Imagine if you just let a little bit of it go, you would be that much freer.

Surrender to the simplicity of your own being and imagine how free your life would be.

The Anger That Inhabits Your Being
27/Dec/2019 10:43 AM

I always find it interesting to observe the way people express anger in their life. It is always a very telling exhibition about who and what they truly are and how they encounter and react to life, people, and reality. During the holiday season, which we currently are in, it seems to be an ideal study ground for the observation of human anger as families come together, some people may get a little drunk, releasing their inner demons, and people that normally do not communicate are forced into conversation.

As we all know, some people are very blatant in their expression of anger. They yell, the scream, they hit. Others are much more sublet. But, however anger is expressed, it is done so based in a very selfish mindset in that the person who is angry is the only one feeling that something and from this feeling they are acting out towards another person or other people.

In life, we have all seen people behaving badly based upon anger. In life, we have all, most likely, been angry at one point or another. But, it is what people choose to do with this very negative emotion that sets the stage for life interaction and interpersonal relationships.

How do you feel when someone becomes angry at you? How do you feel when you become angry at some other person? And, what is the causation factor for the origin of that emotion?

I always find it interesting to watch the expression of a person's anger, especially when the reason they are angry is not clearly defined in their own mind. Meaning, they are not necessary mad at a specific person for doing a certain thing. Yet, they angrily act out towards an individual.

Commonly, people who are harboring some inner anger and are not emotionally evolved enough to isolate why they are angry, and from this they allow their anger to be broadcast to unsuspecting others, is perhaps one of the most telling signs of an anger-driven person. They are angry. They feel the way they feel. The may even know why they are angry in a specific moment at a specific person but they are not emotionally in control of themselves enough to learn a way to coup with their anger in a constructive manner so they allow it to bleed out onto people that have nothing to do with the actual causation factor of their anger.

Personally, I have encounter people who have said mean things to me, some have even blown up and try to start arguments with me, or they have simply thrown unfair or untruthful appraisals of my life at me based upon unanalyzed anger as a means to start a fight. Later, they would say that they were angry and behaving badly due to the fact that they were locked into a bad relationship and it was causing them to lash out. Okay...

Bad relationships, on the personal or professional level, are obviously a causation factor for life anger. And, in many cases, for various reasons, these relationships are hard to leave behind. But, instead of finding a positive way to deal with and disperse that anger, I have witnessed many people allowing that anger to come to control their social interaction causing them to treat people, who have nothing to do with the cause of their anger, to be drawn into their realm of negative action. Some people bite the apple and end up in a fight.

Personally, I am always very aware of witnessing a person's misplaced anger and am very careful not to allow myself to be drawn into that realm of anger based upon what they say or do to me for this simply allows them to find a way of unhealthily and hurtful anger release. For if you argue with them, if you allow their insults to penetrate your sphere of self-knowledge, then you give them control over your life, your mind, and the next set of circumstances you will encounter.

I have witnessed as some people eventually come to terms with why they were angry and get away from that bad relationship or find a better self-image and then, for a moment, they may not be so combative. But, in virtually every case of this happening, a month or a year later they return to acting out their anger in a negative manner towards other people. Why do they do this? Most likely it is because of the fact that the sourcepoint of the inception of their anger was never found and treated. They never truly came to terms with what caused them to enter into that negative relationship in the first place, they never truly redefined their self-image, or they were just controlled by an undefined dissatisfaction with their life and, thus, they are simply becoming angry with themselves about being angry and focusing it outward. They are seeking out a new form of undefined anger because they have become addicted to the adrenalizing nature of anger.

In life, we all feel anger. Hopefully, we will not have to be hurt to the degree that it becomes a defining factor of our life causing us to encounter ongoing anger. In fact, though emotional lack of self-realization is perhaps the most common factor for anger there are other, more physical motivating factor, as well. I know, due to my own life experience, I was driven into a space of anger due to physical action in my younger years.

When I was twenty-one a woman ran her Mercedes into my motorcycle and I flew face first over her car into the pavement. Back then, we didn't wear helmets, so my skull was fractured in numerous places. For a time the doctors thought I was going to die. But, I did not. What no one told me was when you encounter that type of frontal lobe brain trauma your reactive emotions are really out of wack. Had one of the doctors explained this to me I may have been better equipped to control my responsive emotions more completely. From this, for a time, I expressed deliberate anger. Though not necessarily based in a lack of emotional self-understanding, I nonetheless acted out on my anger. Combine that with previous car and motorcycle accidents and receiving head trauma due to my years in the martial arts and I was the ideal candidate for bad behavior. That was my excuse. But, an excuse was all it was. Luckily, the punk rock era was happening at this same time period and violence was everywhere so I had my outlets.

The fact is, I have known several people who have encountered similar life altering motorcycle, car, and brain trauma incidents. Some had memory loss but most became very reactive in terms of expressing anger. And, this is the problem with life, in terms of anger and anger management, sometimes life deals you a bad hand and you are left being the only one trying to figure out what you must do next. Several of the people I know, who have encountered this type of life alteration situation, remain very emotionally reactive which has led to explosive relationships and deteriorating friendships. Some like me, once they understood the parameters, learned new methods to coup. But, it is not easy.

This is the thing about anger, most people simply feel it, and though they may even know why they are angry and who they are angry at, they never trace their anger to its source and emerge in a place where they can control it as opposed to it controlling them. Thus, their entire life and all their life relationships become defined by anger. From this, many people live a very dismal, out of control, existence.

As anger is a natural emotion, and we are all, most likely, going to encounter it in one form or another as we pass though life—and as anger can lead to some very bad things, it is essential that we must always keep our anger in perspective. We must control it and not let it control us.

If you are feeling anger, trace it to its source. Know what you are truly angry at. Know what is the actual cause of your anger and strive to come to terms with it. Certainly, every now and then, people are going to do stupid things to you—when you are driving and stuff like that. And sure, those actions may piss you off. But, those are momentary things. In five minutes they will be forgotten and your anger will have dissipated. This is the same with people—even your family and friends; they are going to say and do stupid things to you every now and then. But, don't give them the control over you and become reactive to the undefined emotion of anger. Be more then them. Be more than that emotion.

Anger is not a good thing. Anger should not be allowed to control you. Anger should not be the defining factor for the emotional development of your life and your relationships. If you feel ongoing anger, and if it is defining your life and your life interactions, follow it to its source and cure your anger. Ask for help if you need to but find a way to cure your anger. Because a life defined by anger never leads to good things.

Free yourself from anger.

Getting What You Want
and Giving What You Have To Give
26/Dec/2019 08:04 AM

As we have just passed Christmas Day and as we are coming to the end of the Season of Giving the thoughts of giving, gifting, and even wanting are clearly in the forefront of the mind of many people. Each year, as the holiday season approaches most of us are bombarded with thinking about what we will give to this person or that and for some even making a list of what they want and telling people what they want them to put under their Christmas tree.

I always think back to this one relative who used to make up their Christmas list each year and fax it to everyone with the hopes of getting everything they wanted. I always found that amusing. But, times go on, people grow up, they have their own kids, and then, oftentimes, (but not always), the thoughts of who they must focus upon shifts to their children.

In life, we all want the things that the want. It is an interesting thing I believe because most of us believe that if we get what we want our life will become better. Don't you feel that way? As we pass through life what we want changes, of course, but what we want is forever at the forefront of our mind.

I think to a couple of interesting things that happened to me recently in regard to wanting and/or giving…

A couple of weeks ago I was at this flea market/swap meet (I go to them whenever I can. Love 'em! You never know what you will find.) Anyway, I walked past this one guy's space and he was selling this vintage Teac 4-Track mixer. It was the one I really wanted back in the late '70s but could never seem to afford. Back then, I had a Dokorder 7140 4-Track reel-to-reel. It was one of the first prosumer 4-Track reel-to-reels introduced to the market. It changed everything to be able to record multi-tracks at home. I would mix down my music to my Marantz 5220 Cassette deck. I also used those decks to record Swami Satchidananda's lectures. So, they would travel with me. (Wish I still owned them). Though I had a mixer, (a much cheaper one), I really hoped to get that Teac as I knew it would make everything better. But, I never did. Anyway, I asked the guy about it. He claimed it worked and he was asking $80.00. I have a price point for vintage electronics, because you never know if they are going to work or not, (no matter what the seller says), and that price was too high. So, I walked away. But, each time I started to walk away he lowered the price until it got to $20.00. Sold!

I took it home. Hooked it up. It worked. Hooray! I finally got one! But, all these years later, technology has changed so much, I do not even know what I am going to do with it. That is not to say that it is not fun to finally own one. But???

Another thing that happened to me on Christmas Days was… I am a bit of a bibliophile so I have alerts set up to let me know if someone is offering certain books I am looking for on eBay. I checked my online stuff in the AM on Christmas and someone was selling this rare Ram Dass book. I grabbed it up immediately.

As I just mentioned in a recent blog, sadly Ram Dass passed away a couple of days ago. So, I felt like it was a gift from him from the great beyond. Thank you! I know that is Magical Thinking and I always speak out against Magical Thinking but I have come to notice that when someone passes away that you are or were close to it seems like if you a thinking about wanting something, somehow you get it. I don't really have an explanation for that but I would say be careful what you are desiring when someone you know dies as you just may get it. Anyway, glad the book is on its way!

This is the thing about wanting and desire… And, it is something that I often talk about. You have to want what you want or getting it means nothing at all. I mean, most people were just walking right past that Teac mixer and didn't even know or care what it was. It's like at Christmas… For many, they are required to give gifts to people. But, like I always jokingly say to my lady on Christmas morning, *"Here's a bunch of stuff that you don't even want."*

A lot of people only care about what they want and they are only happy when they get that something. Sure, they want it. Sure, you want what you want. But, isn't the important thing that someone cares enough to give you something. …That they care enough about you to reach out and think, *"Thank you for being in my life. I love you. I care about you. Thank you for helping me be a better me."* And, stuff like that…

Caring enough to give is the ultimate gift. It doesn't necessary matter what you give as long as you give. It can be a thing—even that big something that the person really wants, or it can be just a kind word. It can be anything! But, it is really important to reach out to the people that have meant something to you (small and large) and give them

124

something—do something for them because this makes everything better and it makes everyone feel better. And, don't you want to make everything just a little bit better?

Give.

Ram Dass passed on yesterday. I understand that most people who read this blog probably don't even know who he was but he was a very important figure in Modern Western Spirituality. You should check into him. He was one of those few people who came along and truly was the impetus for a change in not only spiritual understanding in the West but the generalized understanding of mind expansion and consciousness, as well.

I know most people don't really care about refining their consciousness, but there are those of us who do. That's why religions like Christianity are so easily practiced. They don't require much. All you have to do is (maybe) go to church on Sunday and pray before you go to bed or when you need or want something. But, truth, consciousness, god, self-realization, and enlightenment require more than that and few people have the voice to guide people in a manner that can be understood by those who aren't really ready to take that deeper step into Sadhana (Spiritual Practice). Ram Dass was one of those few people who actually devised a method to make the everybody understand.

I am sure he was ready and willing to go when his time came. He had spent his life investigating the various realms of reality and consciousness. But, just like when we are born it is one of those shocks of transition, I am sure death must be like that too.

You know, in life for each of us there are those few people who really help us become who we become. In my life there were a few of those individuals. With their passing, I feel a loss because what they had to offer would no longer be new, at best it would only be what already was. Ram Dass was one of those people for me, as was Swami Satchidananda, Thich Thien-An, Bukowski, my puppy when I was a child, and my first cat.

Ram Dass was the first spiritual teacher I ever wrote a letter to when I was an aspiring teenager. When he wrote me a response I was so surprised that someone of his caliber would even care enough or have the time. But, that is who he always remained, someone who helped to usher those with the mind for it into a new understanding of life.

We are all going to die. For some of the great and creative thinkers it is just somehow more sad as they offered so much and now their voice is silent, only remembered by those of us who cared enough to care.

Keep the ones you care about close. Live every moment you can to the fullest with them for someday they or you will be gone and life will be that much less.

Most people don't study their life. They don't follow the path of their actions. They just react to the way that they feel and from this their destiny is set into motion.

Every action you take has a reaction. Every action you take sets a reaction into motion. How you react to the way that you are thinking, feeling or not thinking and feeling causes the next set of circumstances to be set into motion in your life.

How much time to you spend pondering how what you are doing is affecting your life? How much time do you spend charting how what you do affects the life of someone else? And, do you even care?

How much time do you spending observing the way that someone else reacts to what you have just done? Do you ever take the time to take that other person into consideration before you act or you react?

We are all surrounded by a million personalities all of the time. Most of these personalities are lost solely into only thinking about themselves. This manifests in many ways. But, all of these manifestations are based upon a person only thinking about himself or herself and not taking anyone else into consideration.

Driving, for example, is an idea place for the study of human nature and action equally reaction. Think how many times a person has cut you off while you're driving down the road because their mind was lost in the somewhere else and they were not consciously studying their environment. Think how many times a person has been backing out of a parking spot and they almost hit you or your car because they are not consciously focusing on driving and are not fully aware of their environment. Then what happens? In many cases you (and I am using YOU as the you of the greater whole) you get mad, yell something at them, maybe flip them off, and so on. Then what happens? In many cases, due to the fact that the person who created the situation is so lock into a mindset of Selfish Self or Generalized Anger they get mad at you for being mad at them and then who knows what happens next, possibly all kinds of melodrama. I have seen fights break out due to just such a circumstance.

Okay, here's the equation... A person did something. They did something wrong that was their fault. You get mad at them. They get mad at you for being mad at them and the only outcome is a worsening of everybody's everything.

But, can you be more than that? Can you stop the reaction to the action before it leads to all-around bad?

I know it's hard. We all get pissed off when people do something stupid, unthinking, hurtful, or wrong to us. But, can you control your emotions? Are you strong enough to control your reaction to their action?

Think about it... Somebody does something unconscious, hurtful, or stupid to you and instead of getting mad and taking countermeasures you just smile. If they see you, if they look at you, you give them a nod, a wave, and a smile. What have you done? You have tuned the entire situation around. You have made a negative a positive.

Like I always say, if you have done something that has hurt someone you really need to do all that you can do to fix it for a long as that hurt is present in that other person's life not only does that hurt you have unleashed define your life but it also defines your karma. You may not be impacted by that negative karma today or even tomorrow but as long as that hurt is radiating out there, you will encounter its vengeance.

This is the same for large things and it is the same for small things. What actions you enact causes reactions. But, the truth of life is you have a choice about what actions you unleash, you have a choice about what reactions you release.

With all things in life you have a chance to make things better and you have a chance to make things worse. Many/most people are so locked into a space of selfishness that they do not even take the feelings of the other person into consideration, thus all of the problems with this life and this world are unleashed. But, you don't have to be that person. You can smile and be nice whenever someone does something stupid to you. From this, everything becomes just a little bit better.

It takes practice but it can be done. Try it and witness the results.

*   *   *
22/Dec/2019 07:26 AM

Do you immediately dismiss the simple words of
wisdom that, if you listen, you can hear all around
you?

Do you mentally or physically argue the point with
everyone who writes or says something of a
philosophic nature?

Do you think you know more than those who live
their life by a philosophic code different from your
own?

Does the simplicity of obvious truth make you
angry?

Do you hide from the truth of who you are and what
you have chosen to do by living behind the guise of
denial, deception, and argument?

Or, do you simply give into the truth that wisdom
and understanding are everywhere and all you have
to do is open your mind and your heart to
understand that life does not need to be a judgment
based completion, you simply must accept that the
most obvious truth is the most simple truth and the
moment you stop lying about who and what you
truly are and what you have actually chosen to do
and start acting from a more refined and accepting
state of mind then all life falls into a perfection of
refined and accepting understanding?

20/Dec/2019 09:33 AM

Whatever you see is only what you see.

*　　*　　*

When you say or do something that goes against someone's religion do they have the right to punish you?

When someone says or does something against your religion do you have the right to punish them?

*   *   *

Freedom of speech is only free as long as what you say doesn't hurt anybody. The moment you say something that hurts someone karma is created and it will be focused on you.

*   *   *

19/Dec/2019 02:06 PM

What is keeping you from becoming all that you hoped you would become?

19/Dec/2019 02:05 PM

A person only loves you as long as they need you or they want you.

Life, Filmmaking, and Taking Zen
into the Moment
19/Dec/2019 08:19 AM

At the core of Zen is understanding that life is lived in the moment. Where you are, what you are doing, wherever you are doing it, that is your moment. That moment is whole, total, and complete onto itself. That moment is the perfect moment because in that moment where you are is where you are and what you are doing is what you are doing. You may love or you may hate where you. You may love or hate what you are doing. But, all that is simply Mind Stuff based on your own mental definition of that moment. The fact is, however, no matter how you are feeling about that moment, that moment is where you find yourself—it is what you are living, and once that moment is gone, it will be gone forever, and you can never recapture it.

As life is lived in moments, each moment is pure, total, and unique onto itself. Where you are right now, what you are doing right now is wholly pure, total, and unique. Whether you are sitting on a chair you've sat on a thousand times before or you are in an environment you've seen a thousand times, if you look, if you see, if you listen, this time is totally unique from the last time. In fact, it is totally different and unique from just a few moments ago.

Knowing that each moment is pure and unique onto itself, this tells us that we should study each moment, as it will only last for the briefest of times. Whether you do this by simply taking the time to stop your mind and become aware of the uniqueness of the moment or if you try to capture it in some manner, this simple practice can become one of the purest forms of meditation.

In today's world, pretty much everyone has a means of capturing their moments via their phone. We have reached a very unique time in history in that you can photograph or film a movie of your moments and either hold them for later study or present them to the world in the blink of an eye. This is what I have done in my, *"Zen Film, Movies in the Moment."* I see something, I experience something, I film something, and then I present it to the world. ...A unique moment, seen only by me, but presented so that others may study the subtitles and the meditative aspects of that moment. You can do it too. Anyone can... Anyone can take the time to witness the perfection of their moment, see it for the uniqueness that it possesses, use it as a means of meditation, and then capture it for others to study later.

Try it and you may discover a whole new understand of reality, meditation, life, and Zen.

*   *   *

How do you measure goodness?

There's this one market that I go to sometimes that has a business model of selling natural food offerings. From this, the people that work there I would define as being Old Hippies and/or Nuevo Hippies. ...Not the kind of people you find working at a normal supermarket.

In any case, I was in line checking out today. There was a lady in front of me. I had placed one of those divider bars between her groceries and mine. No big deal... I noticed, however, that the cashier did not ring up the salsa the lady was buying. The first thought through my mind was, maybe she wanted to pay for that separately or something. Again, no big deal... The cashier thanked the lady, rang up the salsa, moved the divider bar over to the side, and grabbed one of my items. *"That's not mine,"* I tell her with a smile. *"Is this yours,"* she annoyingly asked the lady that had already paid. It was. *"It was on the wrong side of the divider,"* exclaims the cashier as she rung up the salsa and told the lady it would $4.75. The lady smiling looks at me, shaking her head as she reinserts her ATM to pay for the salsa. I smilingly said, *"No, it wasn't on the wrong side of the divider."*

Now, all of this is no big deal one way or the other. ...One of those meaningless moments in life that fades from memory very quickly. But, it does illustrate a very important point in human psychology. That point is; people lie.

People lie all the time. Many times, just like in this situation, people lie for no reason.

140

The cashier knew what she had done. But, due to whatever logic was going on in her brain, (known only to her own mind), she did not want to own what she had done. She wanted the blame to fall somewhere else. Why? No one will ever know. The thing is, lying like this goes on all the time. Like I have long said in regard to filmmaking, *"What is the number one rule of filmmaking? Everybody lies."* But, not just in filmmaking, lying is rampant everywhere. And, many people lie for no reason.

Have you ever been lied to by somebody? Most of us have and it doesn't feel good when we find out.

Have you ever lied to someone? Most of us have. Did you care about the affect that your lie may have had on that person?

Has someone ever lied about you? Told an untruth about you that ended up hurting your life or your relationships. That has happened to many of us.

The thing is, a lie is never the truth. Yet, because it is spoken it may be believed.

Had I not said something to the lady in front of me in line, she may have believed the lie the cashier had spoken.

The lie was no big deal in the grand scheme of life but it still was a lie and some/many/most lies are not that innocuous.

Due to my life experiences I tend to be less than trusting of most people. That is not to say that I don't look for the goodness in everyone. It is just that I have found that I must be guarded. Why? Because people lie. Some people lie to get something that they want out of you. Some people lie because they want to look like something more than they actually are. Some people lie because they want to hurt you or someone else. Others lie for no reason at all.

Whatever the case… Whatever the motivation for the lie… A lie is a lie is a lie. It is not the truth. If you cannot speak the truth in all life situations, if you cannot be truthful about all of your actions, if you cannot be whole enough to understand that even the smallest lie has the potential to hurt someone, then you should just be quiet and not say anything at all.

Has somebody ever done something to you that really hurt you and, from that action, you are torn apart inside but no matter how sad or angry you are there is nothing that you can do to change what they have done?

Have you ever been really upset at someone on something because that someone or something has hurt someone you care about? You are really boiling inside but there is nothing that you can do that will change what happened to that person you care about.

Look around you. Look at the world. How many people are in pain? Watch the news and you will see wars in distant lands, soldiers being sent to those lands and being killed or receiving life-long injures trying to protect people they do not even know. Yet, the people they are trying to protect are still suffering. Watch documentaries about the life of people in developing countries and horrible things are happening to innocent people everyday brought about by the actions of those possessing some sort of power. Look to people living in your own land, the person living down your street, being hurt by someone or something that they never invited into their life and there is nothing that they or that you can do about it.

Then there is love... Think how many people have fallen in love only to be emotionally destroyed and otherwise hurt by the person they hoped they would happily spend the rest of their life with.

Think about the harsh words or the underhanded actions that you have received delivered by someone you do not even like. Think about all the pain that is enacted by the selfish, the unthinking, and the uncaring and then what do they do once they have created the damage, they either claim the person deserved it or they say that they do not care about that person at all—why should they?

There is pain. There is hurt. There is life-altering damage going on all around us all the time. For some, they are the causation factor: large or small. How about you? Who have you hurt? And, do you care about whom you have hurt? Do you believe you had a reason to hurt that other person? If you feel that way, did you ever question how that other person is feeling or reacting to the pain you have inflicted? Do you even care?

You may be late for an appointment or for work but who but you really cares? Maybe your boss does and then they will fire you for being late. You lose your job. They keep theirs. All that equals is pain.

You want something from someone. You take it. You take it without asking or you take it without caring about what it means to them. You take it, and then they are without it. You have it, they don't. All that equals is pain.

Someone loves you but you don't love them. You do what you do only feeding your own desires and needs then you leave them broken, lost, and alone. Equally what? Pain.

Pain is experienced on the personal level. There are those who create it. There are those who experience it. Which one are you or are you both?

Everyday someone is creating pain for someone else. Everyday someone is experiencing pain. But, just think about life without pain. What brings about pain? It is the individual interpretation

144

of what is taking place on the outside. It is the feeling(s) being constructed by that someone out there and then internalized by the inner person wishing that something was different. Yet, the pain felt is no less. Someone did something and someone experienced that something interpreting it as pain.

The good person attempts to create no pain. The bad person doesn't think or care about the feelings of the other person and thereby creates pain. Some even feel that they have the right to inflict pain. But, what is the RIGHT to create pain? If you believe you have that RIGHT what price did you pay to gain that RIGHT? Who gave you that RIGHT?

Creating pain never equals a good anything. Even if bringing pain to the life of someone else makes the person creating that pain feel empowered, empowerment is based in self-evaluation, it is based in ego. What happens to the person who bases their life upon ego? We all know the answer to that question.

Pain, hurt, and damage is going on all around us all the time. Why is that? Because one person does not take the time to think or care about the person on the receiving end.

As pain is going on around us all the time what can we do about it? The number one thing to do is to create no pain. Hurt no one, no matter what you think or feel about them. Hurting only hurts. It only creates pain. Creating pain only creates more pain. It continues forward.

You want to be something good in life. You want your life to have meant something good. Create no pain. Be strong enough to let the goodness begin with you.

How many flowers have you planted in your life? How many vegetable seeds have you planted so that somebody could enjoy the vegetables that would grow?

I lived in this apartment for a few years. It had a small patio area in the back. Next to that patio was a large square area that had dirt in it. I never really understood why the builders created this area, like a large planter, as nothing was ever planted there.

At one point, I decided to get some flower seeds and plant them in this space. They grew and bloomed and they were beautiful. From that point forward, though the plants were always there, whenever the Spring would come around, these beautiful flowers would bloom. I hope they are still doing that to this day.

So easy. All I had to do was go and buy some seeds, plant them, and the entire world became just a little bit better.

When I was a kid I was given a little patch in the backyard to plant. I went to the grocery store and I picked out some cucumber and carrot seeds to plant. I went home and planted them. With the anticipation that all children possess, I waited for them to grow. Soon enough, small green plants began to appear out of the ground. I was so happy. I couldn't wait until we could eat some of the vegetables I had grown.

A little while later, the plants were in full bloom, but they had not yet produced a crop. The gardener came by one day and thinking that those plants were just weeds he pulled them all out. I came home from school and went out to look at my plants as I did everyday. But, they were gone. I was devastated. I had planted something. I had created something that would produce food but it was ripped from my life and the life of others by the hands of some unconscious person who didn't know, understand, or care about what I was hoping to create.

Back to the question, how many flowers have you planted in your life?

In life, a lot of people do a lot of things. Some people do things for no reason at all but virtually everybody else has logic for doing what he or she does. They can give you reason after reason. The thing is, how many people plant the seeds of goodness in what they do compared to how many do things only thinking about and only to befit themselves?

At its essence, life is very simple. You can either plant seeds that make everything more beautiful and everybody more healthy and happy or you can rip out the plant before it has a chance to bear fruit. Who are you? What do you do?

13/Dec/2019 04:44 PM

Do something nice for somebody today.

Do something nice for someone you love.

Do something nice for someone you like.

Do something nice for someone you don't like.

Human Nature in the Season of Giving
13/Dec/2019 04:32 PM

I forever find it interesting to watch the behavior of other people. You can really learn a lot. You can learn a lot about human nature and you can also learn a lot about yourself. By studying the behavior of other people you can learn the better way to behave as well as you can witness the way(s) you should never behave and the thing(s) you should never do. Watch and you will learn.

It is always interesting for me to observe the behavior of people during the holiday season—the timeframe we are currently within. For some reason, though this is designated as a time for caring and giving, by observing people's behavior, it becomes very obvious that, in many ways, it is just the opposite. A lot of bad behavior goes on.

The porch pirates and the people who take advantage of the giving of someone else, by stealing what they have purchased to be given as a gift, illustrates the lowest level of human behavior. Those people are horrible! But, we all feel that way. Well, at least most of us. …Those of us who would never do something like stealing. But, it is the more subtle levels of human bad behavior that seems to become amplified during this time of year that is more telling about the overall human experience.

Certainly, there are more people out and about during this time of year. That provides us with a greater platform of monitoring human behavior. Yes, a lot of elderly people are out there driving. You know the ones who drive many miles under the speed limit, block other people from passing, and just drive so overly cautiously that they truly create a menace to driving culture. They

149

should really be truthful with themselves and take themselves off of the road. But, that too is an illustration of human behavior. Many people are not truthful with themselves.

I believe there is a lot of abstract pressure put on people during the holiday season. Pressure to give people what they want. And, for some, pressure to get what they want. I think this messes with the mind of some people, making them more oblivious to their actions and, in fact, making them angrier than they normally are as they are forced into the corner of giving. But, if this season brings that out in people, that let's you know who and what they truly are.

If you drive, you may see that a lot of people have their mind elsewhere. Since the dawning of the age of cellular culture, where everyone's face is constantly buried into his or her phone, this has become an epidemic. But, more than simply being focused on their phone, or the conversation they having on it, instead of consciously focusing on driving, many people's minds are lost somewhere else. Thus, revealing the lack of conscious caring that many people possess as they allow themselves to become essentially a driving deadly weapon.

The point I am making is during this time of year, the innate truth of a person's personality is amplified and it comes to the surface more noticeably than may be the case during other times of the year. This can be very revealing about who and what a particular person truly is, as well as it can provide us with a microscope into the lower levels of the human psyche and why embracing and enacting that lower level of consciousness can lead to bad things.

We've all seen newscasts of people getting into fights over more than one person wanting some something at a store. We've all heard about people going into debt by spending too much. We've also all heard stories about people getting really hurt or dying at the hands of a driver who wasn't paying attention or simply was more focused on getting to where they wanted to be than understanding that there are other people in this world.

For example, yesterday I was driving through one of those traffic circle things. I have always thought those things are not safe, yet they continue to create them. There are Yield Signs at every entrance and I was very carefully entering the circle. Just as I was about to pass this one entrance point this lady in her Mercedes, completely oblivions to the fact that there was another car passing within the circle, jams in and if I didn't slam on my breaks she would have a caused an accident. I honk at her, which seems to be the natural thing to do in that situation. She comes to a complete stop and you can see through her window that she is yelling at me and cussing me out. Funny... Yet, revealing. She was one of those loud-mouthed middle-aged white woman who believes she owns the world. The situation was her fault yet she believed I was the one to blame. That was a very illustrative example of people embracing the lower levels of human behavior and not caring or even thinking about the anyone else.

Speaking of honking... I think back to this one time I was on the freeway just before Christmas. This junky old car, full of a family, had broken down in one of the center lanes and had come to a complete stop. This guy driving a Mercedes is coming up fast. First I hear him laying on his horn and then I see a full impact crash. He hit that stopped car full speed. Instead of the guy swerving and getting out of the way, he hit the rear of that car full impact. A lot of people had to have been hurt in that crash, including three children. I believe that most of us would have swerved to avoid impact. The driver, instead, believing he was in the right, or whatever, decided it was better to honk his horn than to try to avoid the accident. Again, an ideal example about how some people encounter life and, in doing so, hurt the life of someone else.

Those are just a couple of examples. But, look around you at this time of year. A lot of people are out there doing. Watch what they do. See how they do it. Observe how they behave. You can really learn a lot. You can learn how you should behave and you can learn what you should never do.

*   *   *

When you don't have anything meaningful going on in your own life you think and you talk about other people.

Where You Are Compared To
Where You Want To Be
10/Dec/2019 07:46 AM

Think about all of the roads that there are in every country around the world. Every/any country you go to, there you will find road after road taking you to somewhere.

Roads travel on until they end. But, where do they ultimate end? Sure, there are a few—a very few that come to a complete stop but most simply feed into another road that will take you somewhere else.

Think about your life. Think about the times when you have gotten into your car and traveled somewhere. You started, you traveled, and then you arrived. …Somewhere different while all along the way there were people living their life. Maybe you saw some of them. Maybe you spoke to some of them. Maybe you did not. In any case, they were there while you were traveling by, getting to that somewhere else.

I used to drive a lot. By the time I was a teenager my friend and I would frequently head L.A. to Vancouver and Vancouver Island. We started out doing the drive up Highway 1, through Big Sir and onto San Francisco. Then, we shifted over to Highway 101 until we realized that you couldn't get gas on 101 in the late night where/when I used to love to drive. Finally, we got it down to a science, Interstate 5: L.A. to Vancouver in about seventeen hours.

There was a point in my life when I used to head up to San Francisco, via Santa Cruz, a couple of times a month. I even spent a certain period of time driving to Vegas quite frequently.

I made the drive L.A. to NYC and onto Montréal more than a few times. Long drive but back then it seemed like there was something bohemian the road had to offer. You know, *On the Road* and all of that...

I think many of us have sought out the, what is out there, by traveling to some place, believing that it would supply us with a dream. Certainly, as a filmmaker, I have met so many people who have driven to Hollywood to live their dream. But, it is an impossible dream and most simply returned home down that long road of return.

There are weird minor memories that each of us possess. You know those odd conversations that were really very minuscule in the overall expanse of our life but somehow they keep popping up in our mind. I think to two of them that were associated with getting to someplace else. Both happened at a gas station out there somewhere on the road.

The first one was with this cute punk rock girl who was taking the money over the counter at a large interstate gas station in the Midwest. I was driving my '66 Mustang, with California plates, and she was so excited. She went into a long discourse about how she was trying to save up enough money so her and her boyfriend could move to San Francisco. She had a gleam in her eyes. You could tell she just knew that all of her dreams would be answered when she got there. But, would they?

The second one was with this the gas station attendant out on old Route 66 somewhere lost in the past. Some traveler was being condescending to him regarding the geographic location. He saw me shaking my head. He looked up after the person had left and said, *"Everybody wants to go somewhere but they never appreciate what they already have with where they already are."* How true…

Most of us, particularly when we are young, want to be somewhere else. We believe if we follow that road, we are going to get there. But, how many people do? How many people actualize the dream that they dream? And, how many people are left disappointed? The thing about the Out There is that it is actually In Here. It is in our mind. …That fantasy, that dream about what it will be… But, will it/can that dream ever be what we see in our Mind's Eye?

I guess for some they do find it. Others just tell stories/lies about the grandness of the Out There. From that, the lie is feed into. The possibly of they did it/they lived it, I can too. But, can you? Honestly… Can you? Is what is promised actually out there or is it all only an illusion of your fantasy?

If we can each just take a moment and embrace what we already have, where we already are, then everything becomes so much better and so much simpler. In fact, it is freeing. If you can love what you already have and where you already are then you have already arrived. Try it. If you are already where you want to be, where do you need to go?

156

The Energy of the Temple
09/Dec/2019 08:51 AM

Throughout my life I have been very sensitive to the energy of places. Whenever I walk into a new space I always become very aware of what the place feels like and the energy that is circulating there.

Every place you go into is filled with an energy. It has an essence and those who walk inside of that energy can feel it if they allow themselves to and be affected by it if they are not aware of what they are being surround by.

I went into this large Chinese temple yesterday, and as I commonly feel in those structures, the energy was very definable—it was very much verging on the negative.

In Chinese temples, whether the deity focus of the temple is the Buddha, Confucius, Tsai Chen Yeh, Caishen, Quan Yin, or whoever, you will see numerous people burning incense and praying. The energy in those places, no matter where you find them in the world, is very much the same. I feel it as very repelling and not a place of spirituality at all. The energy really pushes me away, which is not what is supposed to happen in a temple.

In any case, I was with my lady and I mentioned how I felt about the temple. She exclaimed, *"It's not the temple, it's the people! All they are doing is praying for themselves. I want more money. I want a bigger house. I want more business. Me Me Me! Just like when you go into Walmart, it's the people who make up the energy of the place and that's why it's so terrible to go in there."*

I realized what she was saying was very true. In any space where people embrace a specific type of energy they permeate that space with the energy they embrace. And, if all people do is ask for a certain something then the space becomes energized with wants and desires and pain for not having what they want and desire.

I've spoken and I've written a lot about energy over the years. I've discussed how places like the pyramids in Egypt have been completely robed of any energy they may have one time possessed. Back in the day, I was luckily enough to be able to be the only person in the King's Chamber of the Great Pyramid, by myself, for a long period of time so I was really able to study the energy purported to be there. I've also talked about how there is a lot of very intense energy of gods or spirits in certain areas on the mainland of China. So energy, or the lack there of, is not specific to one region of the world.

One of the main things about energy, and why it is important to be aware of what type of energy is surrounding you, is that if it is negative or bad you do not want it to be able to take a hold over you, even for a moment. Because then bad things can happen.

Think about it... Energy does not have to be some big metaphysical parable. Have you ever gone to a football game or a political rally and everybody is all-excited about something. The people all feed off of that energy and if it is based in negativity then negative things can happen. Just like if it is based in positivity, positive things can happen.

Energy is all around us. Everywhere we go, everyplace we live, possesses an energy. Certainly, you no doubt have walked into certain places and felt a weird vibe. That's the energy of the space. Maybe it was consciously invoked by the inhabitants or maybe it just came into existence due to the erratic energy of the people who live or hang out there. Energy exists everywhere. If you are not aware of its existence, it can take control over you. But, if you are aware of it, if it is good you can embrace it, if it is negative you can deflect it. But, you must be aware and acknowledge that it does exist if you ever hope to control it.

So, the moral of the story, know where you are. Feel what is going on around you. Study your feelings as you react to where you are. Experientially feel what is present in the places that you are. If the energy is good, embrace it. If it is bad, leave or deflect it.

We can't always decide where we will be or where we must remain for a time. But, we should never let the energy of any space control us. We can be the center of the energy, at least in ourselves, and from this we can become stronger and not controlled by the energy of any space where we find ourselves. From this, we will be allowed to be ourselves, who and what we are, and not directed in any direction that we do not truly wish to travel physically, emotionally, or spiritually.

* * *
09/Dec/2019 08:50 AM

What do you ask for when you pray?

07/Dec/2019 07:26 AM

If you hide in a closet for long enough sooner or later people are going to forget that you are in there.

A Little Bit Buddhist a Little Bit Rock n' Roll
05/Dec/2019 04:30 PM

When I was coming up through the spiritual circles in the 1970s it was very common for people to be primarily associated with one group but be very open to the spiritual practices of another. Some people would call themselves a this or a that. Some people would say that they were the student of a specific teacher (guru) but they would be very open to the practices of other teachers and teachings. In fact, they would happily partake. Like one of my primary teachers Swami Satchidananda stated, *"Truth is one paths are many."* Or paraphrasing what Hazrat Inayat Khan stated, *"If you are asked by a Hindu what is your religion, you answer I am a Hindu. If you are asked by a Muslim what is your religion, you answer I am a Muslim. If you are asked by a Jew what is your religion, you answer I am a Jew."* And so on...

Certainly, there were a couple of groups from that New-Age era that held very fast to their teachings. Certain Christian groups definitely fell into that category and groups like the *Hare Krishnas* (The International Society for Krishna Consciousness) were very teacher and teachings specific. But, all of the rest of us were open. We went and listened to the various teachers who were riding the Holy Man Circuit of the time and I believe we believed we learned a lot.

When I was coming up I had a good friend, who I had met at *Hollywood High School.* He walked a similar spiritual path as I did and we spend our time listening to spiritual teachers via tape, chanting, playing our bamboo flutes, going to spiritual centers around L.A. and beyond, and, of course, listening to great music by groups we felt embraced a metaphysical mindset like *The Doors* and the then up and coming *Patti Smith*. As I moved forward to be more associated with specific spiritual groups like the Integral Yoga Institute and The Sufi Order my friend-base increased and we would travel the coast chanting for hours and embracing spirituality in all that we did.

It was really a great time in my life and a special time in history. But, that was a different time. Times have changed. Now, there is so much animosity against people who practice different religions and hold different beliefs. The world really is a mess. Simply listening to what people say about those of other cultures and other religions in places like restaurants or stores and it is really shocking. In fact, it's sad. As I understand several languages, I can tell you, this not simply something that is going on only with English speakers. There is a lot of negative talk from a lot of different people even about the people born here in the U.S., spoken by newly arrived immigrants.

...It's always funny the things people will say when they believe the person sitting next to them doesn't understand their language.

In many ways, modern society, at least here in the West, has tried to be open to other systems of belief. I know in some Western countries they have attempted to ban the wearing of traditional religious garments like the hijab. But, most Western societies are open to allowing people to be who they are, at least on the larger scale. But, who and what they are oftentimes becomes the ultimate question.

For example, there is this very nice young Muslim girl who wears a traditional black hijab to work everyday at this restaurant I frequent. As we all understand Muslims do not eat pig. Anyway, one day I was there and I asked her to grab me one of the Soufflé they had available. I told her anyone would be fine as they all are good. She returned with one that had bacon on it. I joking asked her why she would give me one with bacon as she was a Muslim. She smiled, not really having an answer. Then I said, in Arabic, as I put my hand over my heart, *"La ilaha illallah muhammadur rasulullah."* *"You're a Muslim,"* she exclaimed. *"You're so blonde..."*

So, here's the thing, looks are deceiving... I've talked about times in Israel, Turkey, and Egypt where they would not let me in places specifically designated for Muslims. They see me and they think they know what I am. But, they do not. I was initiated into *The Sufi Order* when I was sixteen years old. *The Sufi Order* is a Muslim sect. But, because I am blonde people think they know who and what I am. They're wrong.

One of the most important things that you need to realize in life is, you don't have to be one thing to be another. You can be more than what you are on the surface. Do I consider myself a Muslim? Yes, I do. Do I consider myself a Hindu? Yes, I do. Do I consider myself a Buddhist? Yes, I do. But, I don't have to wear what I am on my sleeve. I don't have to wear the orange clothing of a swami that I once did. That's all illusion! That's all deception! That's all mind games! That's all let's play dress up! Who you are on the inside is who you are on the inside. And, what you wear may express that but that expression is only part and parcel of the illusion of life, just like the color of your hair or the color of your skin.

What you believe in life my change and it may evolve and it may expand. That's good. That's natural. But, if you don't take the time to study what other people know... If you don't take the time to believe what they believe you can never understand anything because then, at best, you are only basing what you think upon what you have previously been told. You are only basing what you believe on a very limited set of facts. If you are not open to new thoughts, ideas, and beliefs, then you are closed. What does closed equal? Limited understanding. And, limited understanding equals nothing more than judgement, conflict, and war.

You can only know when you know and you cannot know until you have tasted the elixir.

*   *   *

05/Dec/2019 02:53 PM

Ask yourself at the end of everyday, *"What did this day mean to me?"*

*   *   *

You can wait by the telephone all day long but if no one has your telephone number nobody is going to call you.

05/Dec/2019 10:11 AM

How much time do you spend undoing any of the damage you have created?

You Only Get One Shot
AKA Putting Your Ego In Check
05/Dec/2019 09:16 AM

There is this old belief, which is commonly spoken about, that you only get one shot in life. …That you are offered one opportunity and if you don't take it, that's it, it's all over, you'll never get another one. That's really not true. But, what is true is that in one specific situation you generally only have the one opportunity to make your way forward and if you blow that then that one specific opportunity will cast you aside.

I believe if we look at life—if we look at the life of ourselves and if we view the life of other people we can easily see how we (and others) have, at certain times, tossed that one opportunity aside. We are offered a stepping-stone and for, whatever reason, we do not take it.

But, what is the reason for that? Study it and the answer to that question will tell you a lot about your life and the life of other people.

First of all, look to your own life. Think about a time when you were offer an opportunity and you did not take it. Why didn't you take it? Seriously, scan your memories and look deeply inside. Why did you turn it down? Was it fear that you would fail? Was it fear of success? Was it your ego telling you that you were better than what was being offered to you? What was in your mind?

Now, take a look at a life opportunity that you were offered and maybe you begin to walk down the road towards the achievement of that end-goal. You were walking down the road but then you threw a roadblock in your own way. What was the cause of that? Why did you hinder your own life progress? Was it ego? Was it anger that you were not being treated the way you thought you should be treated? Did you think you had already mastered the path and you needed no more guidance, direction, or help making it to the finish line? Again, what was in your mind?

Really... Take a look at your life. Take a look at where you are now. Scan your memory tapes and remember where you hoped you would be at this stage of your life: five, ten, or twenty years ago. Is where you are now, where you wanted to be then? And, who helped you get to where you are now and who caused you to fail in the actualization of your dream? Was it them or was it you?

Now, take a look at the life of someone else. I am sure that there is someone who will readily come to mind that you watched and witnessed as they threw away a life opportunity that they were offered. Remember their actions. Remember their desires. Remember who they hoped to become. Calculate where they are today as opposed to where they could have been and chart what caused them to arrive at the place they are currently inhabiting.

It is impossible to truly know the mind of another person. It is impossible to truly understand why that other person does what they do. But, from an outside perspective you can often see what their choice of action gave to in their life, whose toes they stepped on, and why they have ended up where they have ended up.

Life is a process of learning. Life is a process of desire and attempting to actualize that desire. Life is a process of taking the steps towards and interacting with the people who can aid you in the achievement of your desires. Life is also a process of making choices. This is where it gets complicated in the sense that each choice leads to your next set of available circumstances and if you step on the toes of those people who are trying to help you then you may be left living a life void of what you desired to become.

When you are in the developmental stage of any aspect of your life it is essential that you keep your ego in check. Sure, you may not like what is taking place. You may not like the choices that are being made for you and for others. You may not like the direction of the progression but as you are not (yet) the one in control you may not (yet) have a true understanding of the all and the everything that is taking place. From this, if you act or speak against the progression, or the person who is guiding that progression, then this is where you may cause your own ultimate demise, as without the help and the guidance of those who are in control of any anything you may never be able to reach your end-goal.

If you look to life you see it all the time. There are the people who hope to achieve something and they turn to those they believe can and will help them. Then, at some point in the process, they turn against that individual, believing that they are their equal or perhaps even their better. From here, they step out on their own forgetting about all of the help and guidance that person gave them and perhaps even attempting to soil their name in order to gain some sense of self-suchness. But, follow that person's life down the road, a year or two or ten years later, and what has become of them? At best they are only what that other person helped in creating. At worst, they have fallen off of the map altogether.

If a life is defined by a person's ego, what can they hope to ultimately achieve? If a life is defined by one person's judgment of another, what can they hope to become? If the people who open the door for other people are thought to be less than the person who is walking through that door then what is the state of the mind of the individual who allowed that door to be opened for them in the first place? Who are they? What are they?

In life, we each have teachers. In life, we all have helpers. If you cannot put your ego in check long enough to learn what that person has to teach and receive the help that they have to offer then more often than not you will be left never having achieved all that you could have achieved. If you do not possess the reverence for acknowledging who you gained your what from, than not only does that make you a shallow person, you are all also a liar and a deceiver. Again, what does that ultimately lead to? A life of never achieving what you could/should have been.

In life, be aware of the doors that are being opened for you. In life, be aware that your will not always be the one in control. In life, be humble enough to learn what you can learn from whom you can learn it from. In life, acknowledge whom you gain your what from. From this—from being humble and truthful maybe you can reach the life plateau that you hope to touch. If not, it's all your fault. Blame no one else but you if it was you who caused you to blow your one shot.

*　　*　　*

04/Dec/2019 10:02 AM

If all you have is your opinion then all you have is nothing.

The Realizations
You Should Have Had Yesterday
04/Dec/2019 09:07 AM

I think for all of us we have encountered a life situation when we made a choice or did a something only later to realize that it was totally the wrong thing to do. This is perhaps optimized when we believe a person is one thing and they turn out to be something totally different. The fact is, our entire life is defined by the choices we make and the people we associate with. The problem is, sometimes we realize far too late that we should never have made the choices about life and about people that we have made. Yet, there we are in the aftermath, left only with the what is left and not the what we believe should have been.

In the technology world this is also the case. We learn how to do something a certain way and we do it and we do it. We continue to do it until some epiphany overtakes us and we realize we were doing it wrong the entire time. Certainly, in the arts this is also the case. For the artist, who creates art, they do what they do the way that they do it and like so many people in life they allow themselves to be locked into a structure. The only problem is that may not be the best way for the artist to create and portray their art but by the time they realize this fact time has gone by and there is no way to return to the what once was or the what once could have been in order to redo what was done in the past.

There are so many people who want to tell people how to live. There are so many people who make millions off of writing books and giving lectures attempting to fill that void that exists in the life of so many people, particularly when a person feels that they have made mistakes with their life. But, there is no rulebook for life. What someone else tells you to do is only them attempting to empower themselves by casting their spell over you and as many people as possible. From a person's opinion onto lectures given in grand auditoriums, whenever someone is telling some other person how to live their life all they are truly doing is shifting the focus away from the inadequacies of them self and pretending to be the Knower when no one really knows you, your inner workings, what makes you who you are, what makes you desire what you desire, and what has guided you to make the choices that you have made.

Realizations about life are only actualized by the person who is open to allowing themselves to encounter life in a new, different, and perhaps better way. The problem is, sometimes those realizations come after the fact. …After the fact when you have spent too much money, done the wrong thing with the wrong person, done the wrong thing to the right person, or have simply been oblivious to the truth about who you truly are and what you are actually doing.

There is no guarantee in life that you will ever actually figure it out. The one thing for sure is that throughout your life, in certain circumstances, you will no doubt realize, after the fact, that you should have done something differently.

What can you do about this? There is no hard answer. The one truth is, it happens to all of us. So, you just must live your life from a place of openness to change and realization. And, don't blame others or yourself for the choices that you made when you made them. We all try. We all make mistakes. We all learn a better way to do things if we are open to learning a better way. And, blame of yourself or of others only makes you a lessor person. For the true person, the honest person, the righteous person understands that you only know what you know when you know it. What you didn't know—what you didn't understand, you didn't know or understand.

Don't be angry at yourself or make excuses for what you did, who you used to be, or what you didn't know. Just know that you didn't know. Change the mistakes you made if you can change them. Never make them again. And realize, realization comes when you are ready to realize it. You know what you know when you know it and that's pretty much all you can do in life.

If you have to explain what something is then it is nothing.

* * *

03/Dec/2019 02:24 PM

Can a liar ever stop lying?

Why Do You Have To Be High All The Time?
03/Dec/2019 07:59 AM

The legalization of marijuana has slowly been sweeping across the county. I always thought it was funny, and someone's dark joke, when a few years ago they put it on the ballot here in California but instead of voting YES if you wanted it to be legal you had to vote NO. I laughed, questioning, how many potheads were going to figure that one out? It didn't pass though I am sure it should have. A couple of years later they put it on the ballot again and the law, of course, passed.

There are all kinds of ways you can debate this issue and that's not what I'm doing here. I will say, that as this legalization wave has been sweeping the country it has to drive some of the people who went to jail for weed nuts. I had a friend who did five and a half years in Arizona. That's a lot of someone's Life Time. He got out and died a few years later. All that time gone and for what? Now it's (more or less) legal.

Personally, I never liked pot. It was everywhere around me when I was growing up. Most of my friends, from my early teenage years forward, smoked it. But, all it ever did to me was make me feel like I was going to have a panic/anxiety attack. In fact, I haven't done any drugs in decades.

But, since pot has been legalized, here in Cali, it has almost become this amusing/interesting phenomenon. Pretty much everywhere you go you smell it coming out of cars. People get out of their cars and it's almost like a *Cheech and Chong* movie. You'll be in a store or somewhere and the person next to you will be reeking with the scent.

Let alone the fact that it is illegal to drive under the influence (of anything) but somehow people think that it is undetectable. It is not. It stinks.

But, more than all this, the question in my mind is, why do people have to be high all the time? What is so wrong with their life that they want to encounter an altered reality all the time? Sure, I like a glass or two of red wine or a stein of dark beer but I do not wake up in the morning and need to get high.

The thing is, throughout my life, I have known a number of people who Wake and Bake. They wake up and get high. Some of them stay high throughout the day. But, why? What is so wrong with their reality that they need to get high all the time?

In fact, a few of these people have encountered very negative repercussions due to their smoking weed all the time. Not to mention what weed does to your lungs—and yes it does mess with them. But, some like this one actress friends of mine who used to Wake and Bake for as long as I knew her is now suffering from advanced dementia at a young age. The actual cause of this disease, I don't know. But, putting any mind and body altering substance into you everyday cannot be good for you. Sure, the potheads are all going to argue this fact. Whatever... And, that's not even the point of this piece. The question is, what is wrong with reality? What is wrong with your reality that makes you want to get high everyday?

People do a lot of things to take their mind off of their day-to-day. But, if that is case with you, maybe you should rethink what you are doing that makes you have that need to escape. Maybe you should change what you are doing. For if you love your life, why would you need to separate yourself from your reality and get high?

Helping Those Who Hurt You AKA
Morse Code with the Eyes
02/Dec/2019 09:20 AM

It was the last day of the long Thanksgiving weekend and I was kicking back with my lady watching Sunday night TV tipping back a glass or two of the Italian red wine. Basically, just living like everyone else in the world. After the eleven PM news, at least here in L.A., the minster Joel Osteen has his broadcast on the CBS network and occasionally I watch it for a few moments.

Recently, Osteen has received a lot of press due to his association with Kanye West. For those of you who may not know, Osteen speaks like a Tony Robbins self-help guru with a biblical edge. He speaks about positivity and goodness, so you can't put him down for that.

Last night he was talking about not taking action against those people who hurt you. I think this is a problem that most of us have encounter in life, as it is not uncommon for some people to do some pretty fucked up shit to other people when they are lost in the mindset of hurt or selfishness. And, hurt never feels good or helps anything. Paraphrasing here, like Osteen said, a lot of people go to the mindset of revenge when this happens but then all that does is to tie down their minds into a space of negativity.

From my own perspective, and what I believe most people think or feel, is that when someone does something hurtful or negative to someone else we turn to the hope for karma—they will get theirs. And, they usually do. You can't hurt someone and expect not to be hurt. But, more than that, and the thing that most people never think

182

about is, you can't take revenge and expect not to also be hurt because hurt only hurts and no matter who you hurt, for whatever reason you hurt them, there is damage created and the moment you create damage to the life of anyone you will receive damage.

The sad news of karma is, sure, sometimes people get theirs. Maybe you are even there to witness it. But, the fact of the matter is, even when they get theirs, though that may make you feel a little bit better, that never undoes the hurt that they have done to you. So sure, you can dance around the subject all you want but hurting never helps. Hurt only generates more hurt. And, the karma dealt to one person will only cause further karma to be dealt to the person who did the deal if they attempt to enact their own karmic revenge.

The answer, do not hurt anyone! Never do anything that will hurt anyone intentionally. If you hurt someone by accident, do all you can to undo it. If someone hurts you, turn it all around, do something nice for them. Say something nice about them. Not only does this make you a better/bigger person but it also keeps you from encountering the negativity embraced by enacting revenge-karma.

Just don't hurt people because hurt only hurt. Be more than someone who stoops to that level. Avoid and rebuke those people who do. Make the world a better place one good deed at a time.

As for Osteen, he has found a good way to help a lot of people. He's obviously making a lot of money doing it. Good for him. ...Wish it was me. ☺

But, personally, I can only watch him on TV for a few minutes. If you don't get him on TV I am sure you can find his sermons online but the thing that I find very distracting about him is that while is he talking, with each word he very noticeably blinks his eyes. It is like he is sending out some secret Morse Code. The moment he comes to the end of a sentence, his eyes open wide. Like period, end of sentence! Start of a new paragraph. Then, when he begins to speak some more, his Morse Code begins again. It's kind of interesting. It's kind of funny. But, it just drives me nuts so I can only watch him for a few minutes.

Be positive! Do good things! Help People! Even help people who have hurt you! Turn any trend of negativity around and maybe that person unleashing it and the world will become just a little bit better place.

Anyway, hope you all had a great Thanksgiving! Let's get back to work!

*　　*　　*

02/Dec/2019 06:54 AM

People are only supportive of you when you give them what they want.

How many people have you supported when they continued to do things that you don't like?

* * *

01/Dec/2019 07:00 AM

It is easy to say things but that doesn't make what you are saying true.

*   *   *

01/Dec/2019 06:59 AM

Why do you remember so few of your dreams?

30/Nov/2019 07:50 AM

In life, you can decide to walk to the left or you can decide to walk to the right. The choice you make about which direction you will walk defines everything about what you will encounter.

30/Nov/2019 07:48 AM

The reason most people don't achieve anything in their life is that they make excuses to themselves and to others about why they can't accomplish something.

How Do I Get a Buddhist to Believe in Jesus?
27/Nov/2019 09:27 AM

I was in a Starbucks yesterday, waiting for my latte, and I heard a woman ask a man, *"How do I get a Buddhist to believe in Jesus?"* *"Wow,"* I thought, *"Quite a profound question."* It was one of those questions that reverberated in my brain kind of like a Zen Koan.

I have no idea what caused that question to be asked. And, I couldn't really hear what the man's answer was, as it was kind of noisy inside the shop. But, I think it is better that way. It left me pondering the question with no input on the resolution.

I did hear the lady apologize to the man just before she left, telling him that she hoped she didn't offend him.

Who was he? I don't know? A Buddhist, I guess. Who she was and why did she asked the question, I will never know. But, all that is okay too.

I believe if we look to the root of this question, many things can be realized. First of all, and perhaps most importantly, why would someone want to make a Buddhist believe in Jesus in the first place? The two religions come at Universal Truth from a completely different point of view. But, what this does illustrate is the very common practice that Christians want to convert other people to their religion believing that theirs is the only true way. Buddhism, by its very design, is not like that, however. Converts or the number of converts do not make a religion. It is only the true believers that define a religion and attempting to make someone else believe only pollutes the spirit of the religion because at the heart and the soul of any person is the religion that they were programmed into in their infancy. Yes, some people claim conversion. Yes, some people even become Born Again. But, it is at the essence of the being of a person, beyond all outward claimed beliefs, that is actually who they are. Deep inside their inner being is the only place where their beliefs are truly exposed.

If you want to witness what a person actually believes be with them at the time of their death for it is only then where what they truly believe may be revealed.

Throughout the world people believe that their religion is the only true religion. Their god is the only true god. Their practices are the only true practices. Their prayers will be answered and so on. But, true Buddhism is beyond all that. Buddhist don't pray. The ones who do are only delving into idol worship as the true teachings of Buddhism are geared towards the practitioners removing themselves from desire and thus the bounds of karma and reaching a state of interactive enlightenment. Prayer is all based upon desire. What the pray-er wishes for. That is not Buddhism and that is why, for the true Buddhist, they can never be converted to Christianity as at the crux of their belief is not idol worship but walking on a pathway laid down by the Buddha that guides the zealot towards personal emancipation.

Question: *How do I get a Buddhist to believe in Jesus?*

Answer: *You can't.*

*   *   *

27/Nov/2019 09:27 AM

You are never going to know what it is like until you know what it is like.

I have two clocks in my bedroom. One I set via the time on my iPhone, which, as far as I can tell, is the real/actual time. I also have another clock that sets itself via a satellite or something. I actually like that one better because when the power goes off and comes back on it resets itself. I don't have to do anything. The thing is, that clock says the time is four minutes later then it is on my other clock. Four minutes, that is a long time.

I virtually always wake up before the morning alarm goes off. One of the first things I do is to check the time on the two clocks. Then, I lay there. It is a great time for open-eye meditation and self-refection. It also makes one/me become very aware of the unique quality of time.

Think about it; think if you had four minutes to change your life. Think about how long four minute actually is. Think if you arrived at the intersection where you had that car or that motorcycle accident four minutes later. It never would have happened. Think if you had arrived at the scene four minutes later where that person accosted you and started a fight with you or stole your purse or... It never would have happened. Think if you had four more minutes to take that test, you probably would have passed it. And, the list goes on. Four minutes can/could have changed your everything.

It is really important to become aware of time in your life. It is essentially important that you witness it, embrace it, and use it to the best of your advantage. It is imperative that you study it and see how it affects your life. Never forget the essential

life-defining factor of time and how even four
minutes can change your everything.

26/Nov/2019 07:26 AM

Embrace positivity.

See all life events as something you can learn from.

Be nice to people even when they are not nice to you.

Expect nothing.

Smile.

Give instead of expecting to receive.

Only express positive emotions.

Blame no one for your own shortcomings.

Never do anything that will hurt anybody.

If you hurt someone do all you can to un-hurt them.

Say good things.

Do good things.

Consciously become more.

Make the world a better place.

*　　*　　*

25/Nov/2019 03:51 PM

When you make a choice to do something only you are responsible for the outcome. Stop blaming anyone else.

What You Say is What You Become
25/Nov/2019 03:42 PM

The reason people chant a mantra is that it is believed that by continually reciting a holy name the person who is doing this will ultimately merge with the sacred energy evoked by repeating a name of god.

With the power of positive thinking it is taught that by constantly catching any negativity that is found in the mind or in the speech and replacing it with positivity one will bring their life to an uplifted level where good things come to them because they are only thinking, saying, and doing good things.

Karma is constantly spoken about and it is believed that if a person says or does something to hurt another individual they will eventually be held accountable and will be hurt as they have hurt that someone else.

Most people in the world do not think of any of these things, however. How about you? Most people do not chant a holy name in meditation in order to raise their being to a higher state of divine consciousness. Most people do not attempt to only embrace positive thought, speech, and action in order to not only make their own life-experience better but to make the life of everyone they encounter better. Most people do what they do, motivated by whatever they are motivated by, and if they hurt someone in the process, so what! Maybe their action even provided them with a sensation of power or conquest and that felt good! But, when something bad happens to them, they never take the time to analyze why they are being hurt and what action caused them to encounter a reaction.

The ultimate truth is, most people only think about themselves. If they are happy they are happy. If they are sad or depressed they turn to a doctor to give them a drug to fix them. If they are hurt they look to and blame the person who hurt them. They never look to what they, personally, did to set the hurtful situation into motion.

Many people want to be the judge and jury of another person. Many people what to believe that they are right. Many people don't care who they hurt as long as they get what they want. How about you?

In life, what you set in motion is what you will encounter. If you are positive—if you force yourself to be positive even in the midst of negativity, you are a better person for behaving in this manner. As such, all of those people you encounter become better because of you. They feel better. They act better. But, if your life is not geared towards the spiritual, the thinking and doing positive things, the caring about others before you care about yourself than who is to blame when you feel lonely, lost, unhappy, depressed, angry, or you are unnecessarily hurt by outside forces.

The world begins with you. What are you going to think next? What are you going to do next?

Have you ever looked up some old friend online hoping to find out what they've been up but you find nothing? Maybe you looked them up a few years ago and you found something but now all that is gone? You know they lived. You know they were alive as you knew them and interacted with them but now any record of their existence is gone. It has been wiped out.

Have you ever looked up something about yourself online? You remember once upon a time you saw that some thing on there but now it is gone. Where did it go? It has been wiped out.

Sometimes you hear in the news about somebody that did something that somebody didn't like and they were kicked out of a family or an organization. It is stated that all records of their existence has been purged. They lived it, they did it, what they did affected other people, but their recorded history is wiped out. They have created a lie that lives on forever.

Some people lie. Maybe they want their life to sound bigger and better than it is. They tell stories. But, a story is only a story. It is only factual if it was truly lived. Some people lie about other people. They want their life to seem bigger or worse than it actually is. It is a lie, yet it is told as the truth. In some cases, the people who hear the tall tale believe it. So, on some level of reality their lie becomes real as it is believed by others. That story may even be recorded for others to read so it passed down throughout history. But, is a lie ever the truth? No. But, what they have enacted is the opposite of being wiped out. They have expanded on themselves, another person, or a life event and that has caused it to be remember whether what they are speaking is true or false. Do you ever think about this when you hear or read the words of someone else?

Some people lie about what they did. …What they did once upon a time. They did something that they regret—maybe that action hurt them, maybe it hurt someone else, and because of this fact they do not want anyone else to know about it. But, that moment was lived by them and possibly/probably other people. So, it is etched into the *Akashic Record* somewhere in space and in time forever. Just because that person pretends that they did not do that something that they did does not mean that it actually was not done. But, it hidden—hopefully forgotten. Maybe it will be forgotten but does forgetfulness erase the truth of reality? Can anything based in truth and lived in reality truly be wiped out?

Things come and go in life. The knowledge of a person's existence comes and goes in life. The understanding of the truth of what a person did or did not do in life is altered. So, what does this leave us with?

Answer: Life is only truly known to the person who lived it. Who they are, what they are, and what they did is only truly understood in the mind of the person who lived those experiences. As this is the case, attempting to look outside of yourself to the life of someone else only proves to be folly, as you can never truly know anything about anyone else. At best, you can only truly know yourself—knowing what you have lived and experienced in your life whether that life and what you did is known by anyone else or not.

200

21/Nov/2019 06:47 PM

If you want the definition of who is to blame you must ask the question, was it intentional?

Is a Christian who has been baptized by a priest or a minister who has violated children or their parishioners actually a baptized Christian?

*   *   *

21/Nov/2019 01:06 PM

Anyone who attacks anybody because of what they think or what they believe is illustrating that they inhabit the lowest level of human consciousness.

The Buddhist understanding of *Mental Emptiness* is a highly sought after state of being for the practitioner who is truly focused upon liberation. Few Buddhist practitioners are, however, focused on obtaining release from the constraints of the mental burden we each encounter in life on a daily basis. Most, simply want to believe in something and, for them, Buddhism, due to their cultural foundations, may be the best alternative.

In life, how many people have you encountered that seek true mental liberation? How about you? Most people simply are willing to deal with the ups and the downs, the joys and the angers, the happiness and the sadness that normal life supplies us with everyday. Not right, not wrong, or otherwise, this is simply the way that it is.

For the person who does seek a conscious mental advancement, they may turn to various forms of meditation to achieve this end goal. Commonly, in meditation, the practitioner is taught to turn off their thoughts and embrace the silence and the emptiness of No-Thought. Though for anyone who has cared enough to attempt to practice meditation, they will quickly realize that turning off their thoughts and embracing emptiness is not an easy practice. It is for this reason, and others, that I have often suggested that the person who desires to meditate make *Open Eye Meditation* their primary technique. Meaning, instead of attempting to stop their thoughts, a person truly embrace their living experience, in the most refined manner possible, and thereby come to a state of meditation via *Awareness Realization.*

For the person on the path of consciousness, they have entered that path consciously for they understand that it is the only way that one's consciousness may be expanded. This being said, if one is bombarded by thoughts and emotions and controlled by their thinking mind they will, most likely, never encounter Satori.

Yesterday, I had picked up my friend and we were driving down the coast to have lunch. They work in the world of nine-to-five so they have one hour for their lunch break. As I was driving I encountered a very strange experience, thought conscious (as I was driving) my mind had gone completely silent. We were not speaking we just moving in the natural rhythm of life. Eventually, I asked them about this feeling of emptiness and if that is what they encountered everyday during their lunch break. They said that it was. So, like a Contact High this person has passed onto me the conscious emptiness that is so sought after in meditation. This experience was very profound.

For me, I tend to be a very hyper person. *When I am On I am On.* I suppose some would say that this personality trait goes back to my incubation period when after I was born my mother would often brag that all she did when she was pregnant with me was drink coffee and smoke cigarettes. That was a different era... But, just as all of us will-be children are orchestrated while in the womb, I am sure I too, and the personality I possess, was created, at least partially, in that environment. But, moving beyond what was created for me, my mind obviously goes to the pathway of defining higher consciousness. Thus, I am always looking for and always aware of new pathway to achieving that end.

Yesterday, it was as simple as being in the presence of someone who simply completely releases when they walk out of their office. What goes on there is left behind and they allow their mind to naturally embrace profound emptiness. They don't think about it. They don't try to do it. They simply allow it to exist.

This is the thing about meditation and embracing the *Empty Mind* that many people do not understand... Like all prescribed meditation techniques, it is the job of the meditator to put the technique into practice. But, I have long believed that the technique is oftentimes the culprit in keeping one from truly encountering the *Empty Mind* in meditation because they get lost in the technique. But, if there is no technique then the individual seeking the Empty Mind and thereby Higher Consciousness is freed from the constants of the technique that may be holding them back.

So, here it is... Here is your method for the day... Just let go. Let it all go. Let go of your thoughts. Let go of your feelings. Let go of your memories. Let go and know *the Empty Mind.*

The creative process is based upon the artist envisioning an idea and then bringing that idea into reality.

What is in the mind is limitless. There are no boundaries about what can be created. Once that idea is attempted to be constructed in the material world, however, the reality of reality sets in and what was envisioned in the mind runs up against the wall of actuality.

Have you, as a person, ever desired to create something—something new and unique? Have you thought about the creation of it in your mind? Have you mapped it out in your mind? Have you fantasized about what it would be when it was competed? Have you seen in completed through your mind's eye?

Have you, as a person, ever attempted to actually create that something? Have you actually put the components together to give that idea life? Have you actually attempted to make it happen?

For most, creativity is left locked in their mind. They think, they dream, they idealize about the creation they will create—they talk about that something they will create someday. They discuss and critique what others have created. But, they never actually attempt to make their own personal mental vision a reality.

Reality is hard. Creating something is hard. Making something from nothing is hard. Moving something from the mind into reality is hard. That is why there are so few people who may be considered artists in the world for the people who can move an idea from their mind into actual reality are very scarce. There are very few who posses the ability and the dedication to actually transport something from mind to reality.

Many people do many things in life. They do what they do what they do, but why do they do it? What is their motivation? This is the same with the creation of something be it art or anything else. The why is the ultimate question in the creation (the doing) of anything?

Why do you do what you do? Why have you dreamed about creating what you have dreamed about creating? Why have you created what you have created? Why have you not created what you thought about creating? Why is the ultimate question that must be investigated inside of you?

Why a person does what they do is one of the essential question of life and also one of the quintessential understandings that must be possessed if one hopes to walk the road towards self-awareness. Again, most people just do. But, why do they do? Why do you do? What is your intent? Few ask these questions of themselves.

Think about all of the things that have been created in this world. Think about all of the things that have been done in this world. Think about the art. Think about the creations. Think about the doing. Think about the things that people that have done that have helped other people—providing them with joy and inspiration. Think about all the things that people have done that have hurt one or more people. All of these things were first envisioned in the mind of a person and then that idea was brought forward into reality.

Was what was thought what was created? Or, was it simply a thoughtless act that helped or damaged the reality or one or more people?

At the seed of any creation (of any doing) is the intent. The content reflects the intent.

Do you ever study the intent of what a person has done once they have done it? Or, do you simply accept it for what it is?

How about you? Do you ever truly analyze why you do what you and how what you do affects others? Is your inner-mental creation envisioned to help, provide joy, or is it designed to create hurt, anarchy, or destruction?

The fact is, if you do not seek to know the intent of any creation (any doing) many a bad thing has been perpetrated onto the minds and the lives of society.

Seeing without understanding is not seeing at all.

For the creator, know what you are creating and why. Always take the final viewer into consideration.

For the viewer, know what was created and why. Always seek to understand the intent of the creator, for if you don't, a world of illusion is perpetrated onto your life and the life others. And, anything that is done that does not help only hurts.

Always know the intent of the content.

*　　*　　*

20/Nov/2019 09:47 AM

Interpretation is the most factually incorrect method of research.

Lo-fi, Hi-fi and the Essence of Mantra
18/Nov/2019 05:30 PM

There are some people that truly study the essence of sound. They listen for the subtleties of the quintessence of the notes. …Not only of music but for all of the sounds of life. I truly respect people who live their life on that level. But, they are so far and so few between. Most people just hear what they hear. *"Is it loud enough,"* is the only question they care about. But, there is so much more to sound than that.

Sometime I encounter musicians and music creators and lovers of music who truly embrace the ideal embodiment of sound. Some truly try to capture it and reproduce it in its purest form. Those people truly do a service to humanity. But again, few people appreciate it.

Most people only embrace the most rudimentary information that sound has to offer. Do they like the sound? Is that sound pleasing or is that noise? And, so on… They hear it. They like it or not. They forget about it. They never process its subtitles.

Most people are trained not to hear. They attempt to block out the sound whenever possible. They are lock into the thoughts in their mind. Why should they care about the sound(s) that are going on around them?

A lot of people have damaged hearing. Certainly, old rockers, like myself, have damaged hearing from playing and/or listening to music way too loud, way too long. I even had an MRI to study my inner ear maybe fifteen ago or so.

An MRI, that's something I would not recommended to anyone unless it is absolutely necessary. They lock you down on a table and send your body into this very small tube that is only an inch or two from your noise. There you are bombarded with this banging sound of internal x-rays for forty-five minutes or so. Talk about massive claustrophobia. It is so tight there is no way out even if you wanted out. Sure, they give you a panic button but in my case the tech left the control room behind the glass. Who would have heard it if I pushed it?

The doctor said, *"Tinnitus… Nothing he could do. Just live with it as a lot of people suffer from it."*

It always surprises me how whenever I speak with one of my old buds from back in the day, they too suffer from the same thing. It always amazes me. I think I am the only one but it is all of us… And, the kids who blast music through the earbuds in this digital age, they are going to end up no different.

So us/we all have limited hearing though some of us, like me, wish to hear it all. But we, by listening to something too loud, eventually limited our own sought after desire to push deeply into the essence of the sound.

Some people only want the best of the sound. From this, they set up exactingly enhanced stereo systems with perfectly placed speakers. Some buy the highest end earphone, so they are isolated from all external ambient sounds. Some simply want to sit in nature and chart each sound to its source. I am all of those people, how about you?

Most, however, don't care. They just want the sound they are hearing to not be annoying or to hurt their ears.

But, there is something that a lot of people miss. ...Something that a lot of the sound aficionados do not understand. For lack of a better term, that sound is Lo-fi. Low Fidelity sound recordings that were made on not that great of equipment.

Do you ever listen to music like that? Music where it is hard to hear the separation of the instruments or to clearly make out what the singer is singing. Maybe it is just the static-ridden recording of a voice speaking. Though the sound may not be perfect, there is a beauty in the essence of something recoded in this manner.

Musicians and producers spend untold amounts of money to get their sound perfectly recorded so it can be distributed to the masses in its most perfect and pure form. But, again, most people do not care. Most people cannot hear the difference. Most people do not try to hear the difference. But, hearing something recorded in Lo-fi, its substance, its spirit is memorable.

Think about all of this for a little while. Think about how you hear. For this is the heart and the soul of mantra meditation.

What does a person who meditates using a mantra attempt to do? They attempt to become the embodiment of that holy sound. They attempt to climb deep into its essence in order that the sound may overtake their soul. From this, they become one with that sound and the holy purity it embodies overtakes their entire being guiding them towards nirvana.

Right now, take a listen. What do you hear? Think about it. A moment ago, as you were reading this, were you just ignoring it? How about now?

Are you studying the sound or are you just defining what it is and then dismissing it?

Now, try a little harder. What do you hear? Go deeper into that sound barely heard, off somewhere out there in the distance. What is it? Why is it? What is its essence?

Take some time. Study the subtitles of sound. Believe me, it will make your entire reality so much more interesting.

Let Me Jump Into Your Good Fortune
18/Nov/2019 09:17 AM

Success in life is a combination of focus, handwork, and luck. There is virtually no one who has become successful without a good portion of luck on their side.

Success in life is a combination of what you have to offer coalesced with what you are willing to give combined with what you have been given. If no one wants what you are offering then there will be no takers for what you are selling.

The people who are born rich, the people who are born beautiful, the people who are born with some aspect of that undefined something, that everyone wants to have, possess a much easier pathway to success then all the rest of the world's populous that are simply born average.

Some people strive very hard and they achieve success even if they are not provided with the elemental tools that normally lead to success. Name one.

Talent means very little if no one wants to view your talent, if you have no way to exhibit your talent, or if you are held back from performing your talent. But, what is talent anyway? And, who defines who is talented? Name a person who you feel is talented but their talent has not been recognized as you feel that it should have been? Now, think about why that is…

Some people reach a level that may be considered successful. Of course, the definition of success varies. But, what commonly defines success, in the mind of most people, is that an individual has achieved something that has caused them to rise to public awareness, to be appreciated, paid well, talked about, critiqued and discussed by others. Think of someone you know who has achieved this level of public awareness.

Now, think about the people who associate with a person who has reached some level of success. Why do those people wish to be in the presence of that person? How many people can you think of that simply want to be friends with that someone who has risen to a level that is considered successful simply because they like that individual? Name one or more.

Now, answer this question, how many people wish to be in the presence of that successful individual because they want to achieve what that other person has achieved or they want to leap frog off of that other person's fame and connections so that their own star will shine? Think about someone you know who has behaved in this manner. Have you? Have you used the name and/or the fame of someone else to catapult yourself into notoriety or financial success?

Life, success, fame, and notoriety are all defined differently by different people. Many people do not seek fame or advanced life success. There are also a lot who do. How many people do you know, including yourself, who do not want to be the boss? How many people do you know, including yourself, who do not want others to appreciate and adorn them? How many people do you know, including yourself, who do not wish to be financially solvent and live a life defined by no financial worries? How many people do you know, including yourself, who have not sought the help of someone else to achieve what you hope to achieve?

Certainly, we can all agree that life interaction is a complicated equation. From the moment your life begins to veer towards adulthood you are forced into the reality that you much find a way to create a world where you can survive based upon what you personally can and will do. Yes, some people put this off far longer than is morally right by living under the roof of their parents, living on a trust fund, a family allowance, alimony/palimony payments, an inheritance, welfare, and so on. But, most people embrace the factual reality of adulthood and chart a pathway of their own. Some/most look to someone who has achieved what they hope to achieve and then associate with them (by whatever method) in order to use their name, what they know, who they know, and what they have done to move their own placement in life forward. What does this tell us about life? It explains that if anyone seeks you out due to what you have accomplished, if anyone uses your name in their conversations, if anyone wants to associate with you while you are associating with others who have also achieved what you have achieved, all that person is attempting to do is to jump into your good fortune and make themselves better or more because of you and what you have accomplished. How about you, have you ever done this?

In some cases in life, people attempt to hurt other people simply to get what that other individual already has or to arrive at where that other person already is. We have all seen this occur. The people who talk behind the back of others, the people who distort the truth or lie about other people, the people who attempt to diminish the accomplishments of that other person, or the people who attempt to steal the friends or business associates of that other person in order to make their own life better. How about you, have you done this?

Life accomplishment is often made in spite of all the surrounding factors of someone's life. Think of someone who has succeeded in spite of his or her foundational factors.

Life accomplishment is also often diminished by the actions of someone else. Think of someone's success that has been hurt by what someone else said about or did to his or her life.

Most people want to succeed in life. How about you? What have you done to succeed? Who have you associated with in order to succeed? Who has helped you? Who has hurt you? But, more importantly, who have you helped and who have you hurt on your pathway to success?

Study your life. Study your life actions. Study the life actions of others and you quickly realize that virtually no one does anything for no reason. Virtually everybody has a reason for doing what they do. And, that primary reason is that they want to gain something from someone.

Life is a complex pathway. This is especially the case for those who wish to succeed and raise their life to a grand level.

We all need to find a road for survival in life. Many of us wish to be successful in life. But, with any desire for success comes a large level of added ingredients as one walks through their life. With any level of achieved success comes an even larger level of added components, as one must forever be very aware of the motivation(s) of all those they associate with.

The conscious person is always conscious. They helpful person is always helpful. Sadly, most people do not base their life on the perspectives of

218

consciousness and helpfulness—all they want is what they want and they are willing to do whatever it takes to get it. How about you?

So, if you are walking on the pathway towards success, be very aware of who you are, what you are doing, why you are doing it, and who you are associating with. By knowing you, you know what you are willing to do. But, more than that, if you are walking on the pathway towards success, study and control your own actions for anything selfishly or negatively done only equals a diminishment of who you could ultimately become. For hurt only hurts. Taking only takes. Selfishness is only selfish. Uncaring is only uncaring. But, caring, giving, understanding, saying and doing good things, and helping always makes everything better.

Sure, try to become what you want to become but always remember, be the best that you can be in that process. Use or hurt no one. Then, with any achievement everything in your life and everything in everyone else's life becomes just a little bit better.

* * *

18/Nov/2019 07:14 AM

Success breeds an entirely different type of ego.

18/Nov/2019 07:13 AM

Do you ever spend any time thinking about it from their perspective?

* * *

16/Nov/2019 04:32 PM

One of the biggest problems in life is that people do things that hurt other people but because they are so self-involved they never do anything to fix the damage that they have created.

Everybody holds a view about what they hold a view about. People look to others and see where they are in their life in terms of money, looks, fame, and prestige. From this, they draw a conclusion about that person. People look to what someone else has created and they decide if they like it or not. People listen to what others have to say and they decide if they agree or disagree. Most people spend an enormous of time thinking about what they think about that someone else but they rarely study the foundational perspective of their view or of themselves.

Oftentimes, when a person is young they meet an older person and they immediately draw a conclusion about the person due to their age. Maybe they respect the elderly or maybe they just view them as old. Just as when an older person meets a young person and they immediately draw a conclusion about them due to their age. Perhaps they believe that they are young, inexperienced, and have not truly earned the respect of time. Whatever the age-frame, each of these people has not lived what that other person has lived, yet they feel they have the right to define and assess that other person's life simply in terms of their age.

Oftentimes, people see what someone else has created. They then analyze that creation based upon their own spectrum of likes and dislikes. Then, just like in a class in art school where the teacher asks each student to appraise that other student's work, the person disseminates to others their evaluation.

Oftentimes, people listen to those who speak of philosophy. This may be religious, this may be philosophic, or this may simply be what a person thinks about some meaningless subject. They listen and then they decide if that person is saying something that they agree or disagree with. Most, however, are so life-unrefined that they simply listen because a person is speaking. They immediately believe what is being say simply because that person holds the pulpit, thus, they must be worthy of listening to.

When you were young, what did you think of someone who was old? When you see what someone has created do you seek the essence of that creation or do you simply decide if you like it or not? When you listen to someone do you actually attempt to understand what they are saying and why they are saying it or do you simply believe their words because those words are being spoken?

Each of us has been created. No one has created himself or herself. Though some people egotistically hold onto the fact that they are Self Made. This is simply a projection of the ego. Yes, you made think what you think and live what you live but who you are physically, mentally, and emotionally are all factors that were created outside of your own psyche. Though what you like or dislike may cause you to do what you do, at the essence of your being you had very little to do with who you were to become. Your physiology, your physical characteristic, your mental characteristic, your emotional makeup, even your personality were all something that was put into you. You had nothing to do with their creation. So, what are you? Who are you? And, what gives you the right to believe that what you think, feel, create, or believe is any more important that what someone else thinks, feels, creates, or believes?

Some people are very egotistical. They believe that their opinion matters—that it is more important than the opinion(s) and/or the thought(s) and the creation(s) of someone else. But, for the person who behaves in this manner all they are is a projection of their own ego. Thus, they are basing the essence of their life on nothing more that ego-projection. And, what is a projected ego; it is nothing more than a person who possesses an exaggerated sense of self-worth. Thus, the loud should never be listened to.

Before you ever believe that you know anything, before you ever believe that you possess the right to broadcast what you think you know, before you ever believe that you are more than someone/anyone else, know who and what you truly are. The fact of the matter is, you are nothing more than something that was created by someone/something else. So, who are you really? What are you really thinking and feeling and why are you thinking and feeling it? And, why are you doing what you are doing? You are only you in as much as someone else/something else made you, you. So, who are you?

I Never Saw Hell Comes to Frogtown
14/Nov/2019 01:47 PM

People have the wrong idea about me. They always assume that I am a Cult Film Fanatic. Sure, I get it, having been the driving force behind movies like *The Roller Blade Seven, Max Hell Frog Warrior,* and *Guns of El Chupacabra* they believe that is where my filmmaking focus lies. They are wrong. I have never been a fan of Cult Movies. In fact, I don't like Horror Movies either. This is based in the fact that I don't like people hurting other people and I truly dislike negativity being broadcast on the screen on any level. But, that is getting off point a little bit...

For all kinds of reasons, people have long associated myself and my filmmaking with the works of Donald G. Jackson. And, they assume all we made were Cult Films. I get it... But, if you look at the majority of the projects we created together, they were not Cult Films by accepted definition. Yes, they were low budget. Yes, they were shot with no script. Yes, they were shot with limited resources but their subject matter was more mainstream than not. They were based on human interaction and good overcoming evil.

Here's a fact for you, I have never watched *Hell Comes to Frogtown.* Though that movie may be considered Don's most famous feature, that film was taken away from him by the producers and he had very little to do with the feature that was ultimately released. In fact, maybe ten years ago or more, the producer of that film, who was then encountering the fact that he had cancer, emailed me and expressed his regret in that he did not allow Don to actualize his vision for the film. By then,

Don had passed away. Unfortunately, he never heard that statement. I am sure it would have made him feel better because he always harbored deep resentment about what happened with *Hell Comes to Frogtown.*

But, back to the point... I've never seen *Hell Comes to Frogtown.* I've never seen *Roller Blade.* In fact, when Don and I were about to go up on *Roller Blade Seven* we were at a cast member's house and he popped in a video tape of *Roller Blade Warriors* and after watching only a few minutes of it, and not believing my eyes, I seriously contemplated walking out the door and leaving the production of RB7 altogether. I thought it was terrible!

In fact, even the films I produced with Don, but did not act in, if I was not the editor, I have never viewed the finished product. It's just not my scene. Mostly, I hate to be bored or disgusted while watching a movie.

Yes, Don assigned all Rights, Title, and Interest to all of his films to me before his passing. He left me in charge of his filmmaking legacy. And, I have done my best to keep it alive. I believe very few people would have gone to the lengths I have to protect his legacy and keep it intact and alive. But, do I watch his movies or, in fact, any films like that? No, I do not.

Look at my *Zen Films* and you will see a completely different philosophic focal point than most of the films that Don made or that Don and I made together.

I am telling you this story because I want you to know who I am—who I am and who I am not.

I am happy for all of the people that like the movies that Don made and the films that we made together. But, before you can ever truly understand any artist—no matter what art form they embrace, you need to put your assumptions aside and find out who and what they truly are and why they do what they do. I hope this helps, at least in relation to me.

And Then Their Screen Credit is Gone
14/Nov/2019 08:53 AM

The film business is a cutthroat industry. Everybody is trying to get something or somewhere. Whether it is fame, money, power, sex, or prestige, you can get backstabbed in a heartbeat and you will never even see it coming.

Promises abound in the film game. Many people will tell you exactly want you want to hear. They do this to get what you got. Once they get it, see ya...

It is really sad how much of what a person does can be lost due to the selfish actions of the powers-that-be. Screen credits get forgotten or cut out altogether all the time at the whim of the producer or distributor. Editors hack scenes to oblivion completely destroy the overall intention in the move. What can anyone do about this? Virtually nothing. You play the game; you are going to get burned. It has happened to me. It has happened to a lot of the people I know.

I was thinking about a person today that I hadn't thought about in a long time. I really have no idea what ever happened to them or if they are even still alive. I thought the best place to begin my search would be imdb.com as I knew they had written the screenplay for a movie back in the day. So, I went there, typed in their name, but nothing... Then, I popped over to the movie. Gone was their name in the screen credits. Thus, their contribution is lost forever. It has been erased, as at one time I know it was there.

The name that remains in the credits is not the screenwriter at all. It is the wife of the producer. Wow...

So, here is your koan for the day... If you create something but someone erases the fact that you created it, did you create anything at all?

The Art of Positivity
and What You Really-Really Want
13/Nov/2019 01:44 PM

There is always a lot of talk going on about Being Positive and Embracing the Art of Positivity. Certainly, this concept was first highly disseminated by Norman Vincent Peale and the millions of books he sold on the subject from the 1950s forward. Now/today, his name is all but forgotten. But, the subject and the concept of Positive Thinking is one of the cornerstones of many/most New Age, Aquarian, and Humanistic Psychology programs.

But, let's step back for a moment. Think about your life. Think about the things that you think about. Think about the things that you do based upon what you think. How much of your thought process is geared towards Positive Thinking? How much conscious thought do you put into Positive Thinking? In fact, how much conscious thought do you put into anything?

For most people, sure, they know about Positive Thinking and how it is supposed to improve their life. But, do they develop a Positive Thinking process? The answer to this question for most is, no. They live what they live, they feel what they feel, and they do what they do. Maybe they are happy, maybe they are sad, but what they never are is consciously in control of what they are thinking and why they are thinking it.

Conscious Positive Thinking affects the evolution of your life. Unconscious thinking also affects the evolution of your life. To illustrate this, look to the life of people you have known over a long period of time. How has their life changed? Are they who they were when you met them? More importantly, how has their mindset and the way they interact with life changed? How has what they think changed?

Now, look to your own life. View it over a long period of time. How has your life changed? Are you who you were a year, two years, or ten years ago? More importantly, how has your mindset and the way you interact with life changed? How has the way you think changed?

For the most part, what you will realize, when you look at the life of other people and yourself is that, over a long period of time the physicalities of your life may have changed but the you, who you are on the inside, has changed very little. How you view life, how you reacted to life and to others, and how you process your thoughts and your feelings has changed very little. If you were a positive person then, you probably are a positive person now. If you were a negative person then, you probably are a negative person now. If you were an insecure person, a liar, a spiteful person, or an egotistical person, that is probably who you are now. All this being said, what most people never do is to take control over their thought process and choose to not only clearly view who and what they are but then to redefine themselves and their thinking process in order to bring their life to a higher point of mental, psychological, and human interaction.

When people look to their past, most will find that once upon a time they cared about things like fashion, music, and being seen as a cool person who did cool things. Time moves on and much of that falls away. Now, they have merged with the common and though they may remember who they used to be and why they were motivated to embrace that lifestyle and that thought process back then, they have let go of that who they used to be. When people look to their past, most will find that they, once-upon-a-time, held a dream that they hoped to actualize. But, through time and life responsibilities, they let go of that dream.

When someone looks to the life of another person, which in some ways is more easy to rationalize and comprehend, they can remember who that person used to be in comparison to who they are now. Again, what they were on the outside, how they wanted to be seen, and who they wanted to become was allowed to fall away through time. But, who they are on the inside has, however, changed very little.

What this illustrates is how we think leads to what we do and how we behave. But, the fact of the matter is, what we do and how we behave, at least on the physical level, changes over time. What we thought was important then is not what we think is important now. Therefore, why do we allow our random thinking mind to be so in control of our life if what we think and what we feel (what we want to project) will change in time?

This brings us back to the sourcepoint of Positive Thinking. What do you think about and why? Do you allow your random thoughts to control what you feel and how you behave? Do you allow your random thoughts to control what you do? Have you ever developed the ability to control your thoughts? Have you ever even tried?

I believe we have each encountered people who are emotionally out of control. There may be many factors that cause this, but the one common element is that the person does not choose to learn the methods of self-control. No matter what they may gain in life from living in a state of, *"Out of controlness,"* and certain people have gained a lot from this mindset, but even those people never possess the true and deeper understanding of embracing a life based upon consciousness and Positive Thought.

A person who is not in control of their thoughts and emotions does not possess the ability to care about anyone else because all they think about—all they are controlled by is what they (personally) are feeling. Thus, their entire life is based in a random state of ever-changing thoughts, leading to emotions, that dominate their actions in life. Thus, leading to chaos but never focused positivity.

Okay... Again, look at your life. Where are you today? What are you feeling today? What are you doing about what you are feeling today. How is what you are choosing to think today affecting your all and your everything?

Now, think about this, where did you plan for your life to be today; one day ago, one year ago, or ten years ago. Are you where you thought you would be—are you doing what you hoped you would be doing? If not, why not?

Think to the things that you hoped to become. Think of things that you did to reach that goal. Think of thoughts that you possessed in your pursuit of that goal. Did you ever take the time to study your own mind? Did you ever question why you desired that end goal, what you were willing to do to get there, what you did do to get there, and what thought process you embraced in the pathway to your hoped for achievement?

The reason I am discussing all of these various elements of thought, personal appraisal, and desire is that it is easy to see if you think about it, all things in your life begins with thought. All things begin with what you think. But, if you do not know why you think what you think or you allow your thoughts to be out of control and, thus, randomly controlling your emotions, what you achieve can never be based in focused Positive Realization. At best, it can only be happenstance.

As all things begin with your thoughts, what are you thinking and why are you thinking it? What are you going to do about what you are thinking? Are you going to allow your thoughts to control you or are you going to control your thoughts?

The first step to any true Positive Thinking exercise is to consciously know the answer to those questions. It is only at this point that a person may consciously embrace Positive Thinking.

Many people believe that to practice the method of Positive Thinking all they must do is to immediately meet any negative thought with a positive thought. That is a tool but that is only a Mind Game played by the individual who is attempting to mask what is actually going on in their life; what they are doing and why they are thinking what they are thinking. To step beyond the Mind Game and actually develop true Positive Thinking one must first travel to the essence of their thoughts, study their thought and know why they are thinking those thoughts. Only then can true Positive Thinking may be embraced.

Positive Thinking is not Positive Thinking when negative thoughts are simply reformulated as a means of one person pretending to think something different when something much deeper is going on in their subconscious mind. If you want to truly understand Positive Thinking first you must truly know yourself. Then, you must be able to control your thoughts thereby controlling your emotions and your actions. With this, Positive Thinking transcends from someone simply attempting to put a Band-Aid on an uncomfortable thought or emotion and move it towards a pathway to Self Realization.

The Way the Story is Told
AKA Who Remembers What and Why
13/Nov/2019 07:16 AM

Have you ever had the occurrence where you lived though an experience with a friend or a family member and then a day, a week, a month, a year, or a decade later you were with them and they were describing the experience but it was totally different that what actually happened—different from the way you remember it?

Have you ever had the occurrence where you lived through an experience and you were describing it to someone and you changed the actual facts or timeline of the experience in some manner so that the person you are describing it to would either understand the overall situation better or that it would make you look better?

Have you ever had the occurrence where you lived though an experience and then someone who was not even there told the story from their point of view and they either made you seem much greater than you actually were or made you look totally bad? They weren't there. They have no firsthand knowledge about anything, yet there they are telling your story.

I think most of us have experienced this experience. An experience where we experienced something and then when that experience was relayed to someone else whomever was relaying that experience either changed the storyline slightly or largely or we, ourselves, changed it for whatever logic and reasoning we possessed in that given moment.

This is common reality. A moment live and the way it is talked about is always different from the actual occurrence.

What does this tell us? It tells us that people want to exaggerate. It also tells us that people remember things differently based upon the way they perceive the reality they were living. But, more than all that, it tells us that stories about experiences are only that, stories about experiences. Though they may be told in the most truthful manner possible by the person who is telling the tale, what they are speaking about is only their interpretation of an experience based upon the way they encountered that experience and they way they interpret and translate life in general.

You can only know your own truth the way you lived it. What everyone/anyone else has to say about it is only their interpretation.

Know this before you listen to or believe anyone.

People Always Ask Me Questions

People always ask me questions. They ask me questions about my life, what I'm doing, and why I do what I do. That's fine. I'm always happy to answer. I would rather have people hear the truth coming from me, personally, than from some person who thinks they know something about me but what they are saying is totally false or wrong.

Not so much now, as my star has faded, but back in the day, I was asked questions about me all the time. I would get letters, emails, phone calls, people would seek me out, you name it... People who had never met me or spoken to me would also write and speak all kinds of things about me; particularly on the internet. But, so many of those things were wrong, factless, untrue, and biased. It's just not right to do things like that.

It seems that people always have an agenda. That's why I don't like to read biographies of people because the author is always telling the story from a very specific point of view. Maybe they love the person, maybe they hate the person, but what they are saying is, at best, their interpretation of that person and that person's life.

I do, however, love autobiographies. At least in an autobiography you get a person presenting themselves as they wish to been viewed.

I have recently been re-reading Neil Young's autobiography, *Waging Heavy Peace.* I enjoy the way that book is put together in that it is not a linear depiction from A to Z. It moves around. He too speaks, in that book, of how he has sometimes been falsely portrayed. But, he does a nice job of setting the story straight.

Over the years I have thought of writing an autobiography but I realized, the fact of the matter is, through my books, novels, poetry, interviews, and even this blog, my autobiography has pretty much already has been written. That's just who I am. I tell people the cold hard truth about my life. Yet and still, there are those people who do not want to focus on their within—on their making themselves any better, so they talk about me and other people. All they do is focus on the out there—on that other person.

Living life like that is so much easier as they never have to come face-to-face with themselves. This is one of the reason I am not really a fan of most people. So many are so oblivious to their own inner-truth, who they truly are, and why they do what they do, that they do nothing to make themselves or this place called life any better. They just want what they think to be the truth even when it is not anywhere near the truth. They want what they think about that other person to be the truth even when what they are saying is simply false. Truthfully, I don't know how some people live like that but they do.

When the focus is out-there, they are not looking to the in-here and no one is looking at them and who they truly are. That's also why I don't trust most people. Even some of the people I have considered close friends, due to their own undefined self-motivations, have been less than righteous with me.

One of the funny things I find about question asking, and the varying levels of human personality in general is, some people just don't care. I've been with my lady for thirty years and she never asks me questions about anything. She does her and she lets me do me. In her defense, however, I will say that when I bring up some story of my life from the past, she already knows all about it. Hummm???

My father died when I was young. I wish I had the opportunity to ask him questions about his life. There are so many things I will never know. …When you are a child, you just don't think to ask. I found out things about my mother that I never knew just by looking at an old census long after she had passed away. I asked her questions, but she never told me the truth. So, I guess it goes both ways.

What I am saying here is that you and I—all of us really need to ask questions if we want to know the actual truth. If the person is alive and we have the opportunity to speak with them, we really need to ask the questions that we have of them for that is the only way to find out the truth.

Some people lie. That's not good, that's not right, but that is simply who they are. Most of us don't do that, however. Most of us when asked; answer.

The reason I write is that I think it is really important to ask questions of the people you know, the people you care about, the people you like, or even the people you dislike. Most people are not going to write an autobiography. So, if you don't ask you will never know.

Sure, we all think about ourselves. It is us who feels what we feel when we feel it. But, there is more to life than just us. There is our family, the people we know, the people we would like to know, and the all and the everybody that is out there. If we don't ask them questions, when they are gone, all that they were will be gone. It will be lost. If we ask

the questions we have about them, however, at least
then one other person will be able to remember the
who they were and what they lived when they are
no more.

Most people aren't strong enough to change who they are.

The Things That You Do
That Sets Forever Into Motion
11/Nov/2019 09:17 AM

Each action you take in your life is going to set your next set of available actions into motion. Okay... We all do what we do based upon what we believe is the right thing for us to do. If it works out; great! If it doesn't, there is no one to blame but ourselves. That's life. That's personal choice. But, what about when someone else does something to you that changes the definition of your life? What about when someone else does something that changes the pathway of where you believe your life is going? Then what?

I believe that each of us can point to moments in our life when someone has done something to us, out of the blue, that changed the pathway we were walking upon. In some cases these were probably good things. For those things, we are thankful. But, more memorable and life altering are the things that were done to us that hurt our desired life pathway. Those actions are the things that, oftentimes, came to define our life in a much more definitive manner as not only did they caused us pain but they additionally took away some part of what we believed that we were and altered the path we were consciously walking upon.

Why do people do those things to other people? Many will attribute it simply to unconscious action but more commonly it is a method for a person to display some misguided sense of power over another person in order to define their own sense of rightness in any particular situation.

In life, when someone barges in and attempts to control your next set of choices they usually do it to exhibit a position of power. They do it to exhibit control due to the fact that they want to control your life as defined by their own sense of personal righteousness. Of course, a person who does these things to the life of another individual is operating from a very low level of refined consciousness but that does not change their actions and/or how those actions possess the potential to truly damage the life of another person.

I think back to an event that happening early in my life where I observed how the misguided righteousness of one individual altered the entire life path of another.

When I was in junior high school (now known as middle school) I associated with the people who, early in their life, entered into drug culture. At this point we were probably thirteen years old. Anyway, I was friends with this beautiful young girl who had lost a few of her fingers somehow/someway so she rolled her joints by using a small roach clip to put the weed into the rolling paper. She was busy doing that as we were going to smoke out on the school bleachers. Up walks a guy I believed was my friend. He was one of those African-American students who was being bused up to my school, in the Wilshire District, from Southcentral L.A. each day.

He walked up and I didn't think too much about it. He always broke hard like he was some major gangster; so I thought him seeing my friend and I sitting there about to smoke a joint was no big deal. Maybe he wanted to join us? But, the guy immediately went and turned us in. What a pussy.

The gym coach comes out and takes us into the gym offices and the cops were called.

The cops not being that smart or me being inventive, they never found the Whites and the Reds I had stashed in the hem of my sleeve on the army jacket I used wear. Nor did they apparently know what *Blotter Acid* looked like because they took no notice of it when they went through my wallet. They let me go with a warning. My friend, however, as she was the one holding the weed, they arrested her and took her to jail and she got kicked out of school. (Remember this was the early 1970s). I never saw her again but she was very clear that she blamed me for what happened to her as that guy was my so-called friend. I understood her emotions and I felt very bad for her. Her life was changed forever by the actions of that one person passing judgment on what she was doing.

Just a side not here... I have had this weird relationship with Africa-Americans throughout my life. Due to where I grew up they were literally the only people I associated with in my younger years. So, whenever I met an African-American I felt a certain type of kinship with them. I am sure they just saw me as some white guy but the psychological ramifications of my childhood had defined how I reacted to people, just as is the case with everyone. At the time this incident took place, this is when the L.A. Unified School District had begun their ill-conceived program of busing. Thus, a lot of African-American students were brought North to my junior high school, which, in turn, equaled a good portion of my friends.

Where this school was located, on Wilshire Boulevard, created an interesting cultural demographic, as the school itself is surrounded by a very wealthy neighborhood where many of the people live in palatial mansions. Travel a mile or so East, across Wilton Place, and there you found the people, like myself, who lived in dumpy apartments, residential hotels, and boarding house. Add, the students who were beings bused in from Soutcentral and it created an interesting stew of classmates.

...The interesting thing about the whole busing scenario is that when I eventually got kicked out of that junior high school I went to Virgil over on Vermont. That school was riddled with homegrown gangs and violence but the L.A. Unified School District, in all of their wisdom, didn't bus any students there. Curious how they were only busing Southcentral based students to the Wonder White Bread schools...

Anyway... Before I get too far off of the point...

Though what this one student did to my friend and myself was a very clear-cut case of intentional life-damnation... But, think about how often stuff like this goes on all the time? How often does one person, passing judgment on the life choices of another and then taking action on that judgment, alters the life of people all the time? How about you? Has someone done something like that that changed your life forever? Have you done something like that, to someone else, that changed their life forever?

You know, people are who they are. And, people always possess a justification and an excuse for who they are and why they do what they do. People learn and change through time and the actions they take/make are defined by who they see themselves to be and what they believe themselves to be at any given point in their life. All this being said, think about how many lives have been altered for the worst by one person deciding to do one thing simply because they believe what another person is doing is not right or they believe what another person is doing is wrong?

Truly, who holds the right to judge anyone?

Now, I will never know what ultimately happened to my friend. I will never ultimately know what happened to the guy who turned us in. I do know I kicked his ass about a week later. But, the one thing that is for sure is that all of our destiny is highly defined by what someone else has the power to do to us. Though this is not right, this is the way it is.

Sure, there's karma. But, how many people believe they are going to encounter negative karma for damaging the life of someone else when they believe they are the one who is in the right?

Your life is defined by what you choose to do. Your life is also defined by what you choose to do to others. How do you want to be remembered, by what you choose to do with your own life or what you have chosen to do to the life of someone else?

Some people are forever remembered with loving thoughts. Others are forever remembered with disdain. What you choose to do will equal how you will ultimately be remembered.

What do you choose to do, whom do you choose to do it to, and why are you choosing to do it in the first place? Think about this before you ever do anything that may hurt or affect the life of anyone in any negative manner. Because what you do may be remembered forever.

Here is your word problem for the day…

You are driving down a two-lane road. There is a sign that says, *"Road Work Ahead."* There is another sign, *"Single Lane Ahead."* Meaning, the two lanes are merging into one.

Question: Do you courteously fall in behind the car in front of you who is stopped in an orderly fashion or do you swerve into the open lane and rush pass as many cars as possible and then push your way in front of the first car right at the last available opportunity before the two lanes become one?

Think about this scenario as anyone who drives has probably encountered this situation at one time or another. What would you do? What do you do?

Your answer to this question tells you a lot about the person you are and how you interact with others.

One of the things I have been saying to myself a lot over the recent years is that, *"You can't get anywhere in L.A. anymore."* This is largely due to the fact that there always seems to be some form of road construction going on all over the place. In the area where I live, in recent times, there has been a lot of ongoing road construction so I have encountered the aforementioned driving situation more times than I would care to remember. For me, as an observer of life, it always strikes me the wrong way and, in fact, makes me angry when people are not courteous and just dart past the people who are considerately waiting in the line of cars. That's just rude! But, every time I find myself in one of these situations there go the people shooting past in their cars—those who do not care about others, only caring about themselves getting to where they desire to be as quickly as possible—everyone else be damned.

Again, how do you react when you find yourself in a driving situation like that?

There is this group of TV commercials that are currently in rotation that discuss how people eventually become just like their parents. Meaning, they do all the things that old people do. But, is being young an excuse for unthinking, uncaring behavior, especially when it involves and affects the life of other people? Certainly, when a person is young they may possess a devil-may-care attitude. But, who you choose to be when you are young affects who you become when you get older. What you do then set the stage for what you do and what you encounter later in your life. If you don't take other people into consideration when you are young, what will make you change when you are older? And, if you don't take other people into consideration now then why should anyone take you into consideration later?

Your life is based upon what you do. Your life is based upon what other people do to you. Though we can all wish that people will be considerate and nice, that is probably not always going to be the case.

The answer to this word problem... (I guess I should turn this answer upside down like they do on the bottom of those quiz pages). There is none because there are so many people doing so many things based only upon their own specified set of standards of humanity that we are all doomed by the person and the people who only think about themselves. This being said, all you can be is what you can be. The nicer you are, the more caring you are, the more considerate you are, the more people will respect your deeds and perhaps even follow in your path. Then maybe, just maybe, everything gets a little bit better for everyone and people will just considerately fall into the pathway of cars and wait instead of being held back by the people who jump to the front of the line and take cuts.

* * *

If you drill a hole in a piece of wood that piece of wood will never be perfect again.

07/Nov/2019 07:19 AM

When you view a painting do you study the subtleties of the technique used to create it or do you simply judge the content of the subject matter?

06/Nov/2019 09:59 AM

An opinion is not a creation.

Freeing Yourself from the Past
06/Nov/2019 09:30 AM

How defined are you by your past? How much do you focus on your past? How much of your today is based upon your yesterday? How much of your now is predicated upon the definitions you defined of yourself and of your life in the past?

Many people are wholly defined by their past. Everything they live today is based upon their past. Yes, everything you do today will lead to the next element that you will encounter tomorrow but what you did then does not have to become the whole of what you are today.

People look back to their past and base their present on their past for many reasons. Some found a reason for their existence in their youth and never chartered any other road of existence for themselves after that moment. Whether it was a grand moment in school, a something that provided them with an ego-filled moment, a sport that they loved and never stopped being obsessed by, a profession that they began when they were young and never left, or a love that they once felt, a long-long time ago, that they have continually attempted to re-find.

Some people also base their present on the negative aspects of their past. Something bad happened to them back then and they have never let that something stop defining their future. Whatever the case and/or the situation some people hold onto their past and make that time, in the long time ago, their entire reason for being.

We all have memories. These memories form the building blocks of our lives. We all have had situations that happened to us, way back in the way back when, that charged the course of our life forever. This is natural. What some people do, however, is they never let go of those moments from the past and they allow them to dominate their entire future. How about you?

Once upon a time, the past was allowed to be the past. What you lived, you lived back then, and if you allowed that experience to fade, in time it would eventually be forgotten. Since the dawning of the age of the internet, this forgetfulness has become much harder to actualize as not only are so many life-things put out there by the people themselves but everyone has an opinion about everybody else so they say things (true or not) and these comments are then locked into a digital eternity. Thus, it is hard for anyone to leave their past behind and move into a totally new anything.

Me, I have always strived to not let my past define my future. Yes, like everyone, I have lived what I have lived, maybe I have even written about it, but what I was back then is not the definition of who I am today. Yet, I find virtually everyday someone wants to cast his or her definition onto me and tell the world who or what I am. This happens to many-many people in many-many ways. But, all this does is to lock someone/anyone (you) into one point in history—a point in history which has already become the past.

Think about it… Who are you today? How is what you lived back then shaping and defining who and what you currently are? How do you allow your yesterday to make you who you are today? Moreover, what do you do/what have you done to lock other people into their past and not let them meet a new day in a new way?

We are all in control of our own lives. We all have the ability to meet a new day in a new way and not be defined by who we used to be. Yet, in this day and age—this point in history, many things and many people attempt to hold us to our past. But, it is only we, as a personal person, who can take control of our mind, our thought patterns, and the life definitions that we have currently defined for ourselves and move into a new space of existence by embracing the new.

It is only by embracing the new and the different that we can ever move forward in life into new dimensions, experiences and understandings. Don't be defined by your past. Don't define others by their past. Let the now be the new and find and develop new realities for yourself.

There is this homeless guy who has been living in his van in the parking lot of this store I go into periodically. L.A. has been overwhelmed by the homeless crisis over the past few years.

In any case, ever since he moved in and I first noticed his van it always reminded me of my Dodge van that bought new back in '78. This guy's van is a similar color of metallic blue and from the same era.

'78, that was back in the heyday of van culture here in So. Cal. and I guess the rest of the States. I carpeted the back of it and my friends used to refer to it as *The Dodge Motor Inn* due to all of the various forms of debauchery that took place in the back of that van. But, I also would chauffeur my *Integral Yoga Institute* friends between L.A. and San Francisco in it if our guru, Swami Satchidananda, was up in the Bay Area and wanted us up there. It also would transport all of my sound gear whenever I would do the sound for his lectures up and down the West Coast. Plus, I traveled in it quite a bit between Cali and Canada and stuff…

Anyway, I miss it. Different era, different time. Gas was a lot cheaper back then.

Today, as I was walking between my car and the store I noticed that the guy who was living in his van was sitting in the passage seat staring into the outside mirror on the passenger side. He seemed very intense in his gaze. As he's probably a little bit mentally ill I didn't give it too much thought. As a left the store, a short time later, and again passed his van; I noticed he was still staring deeply into the mirror. It got me to thinking…

You know, there is a very specific meditation technique where one is taught to stare deeply into a mirror for a long period of time. It is supposedly designed to cause the practitioner to separate from their ego by embracing their ego.

I've never been too much into that kind of mind games meditation. I mean, you stare long enough at anything and you are going to see weird stuff.

But, more than that, I got to thinking how this guy rarely leaves his van. I mean, wherever I go to that store I see him there inside of the van. How different is what he is doing from that of a yogi who sits in a cave and meditates all day long?

In India, I have met more than a few sadhus who have spent much of their life meditating in a cave. They are all highly revered and considered to be saints.

Now personally, I don't know... For me, meditation has always been about merging the subconscious, meditative mind with common day reality. I mean, I think there is just way too many ways to got lost in the weirdness that anyone's mind can produce if you do nothing but sit alone in a dark cave, day after day, year after year, climbing back into your brain. Sure, you may see all kinds of weird somethings... But, that's all in your mind. Who knows how much of that is real and how much of that is simply projected insanity? And, how does doing that help you and/or the world?

But anyway, this guy sits in his van—his van cave. Sure, he's a little weird. But, how is some guy who decides to sit in a cave cross-legged and meditate for the rest of his life any different just because religion tells him that what he is doing is somehow holy?

Whenever you see what you see, whenever you think you know what is gong on, it's really important to rethink your drink because what you are seeing and what you are thinking may be totally wrong. It may just be your interpretation and your interpretation may be wrong. Maybe that guy who lives in his van is a meditative saint. He just can't find a cave to live in so he's got to live in his van in a parking lot in a big city as he meditates while staring into his mirror.

Have you ever taken the time to observe the patterns of your life? What you do, how you do, and why you do it? If you do, for virtually everyone, what you will find is over time very little will change. Yes, with time and with age and with developed relationships your life placement or your life material well-being may change but thought these outward physicalities may change, you change very little.

Many people never take notice of themselves. They never study the why and the how and the way that they do things. They are too busy living their life to take a conscious notice of what is going on with them and how what they do affects others and their overall life environment. In fact, due to this generalized oblivion many people do not even care—they never give it a thought throughout their entire life. From this, they do what they do to whom and what they do it to—some people they help, some people they hurt, and there overall life excels or diminishes but at the end of the day all they are left with was and is who they always were. They have never evolved.

Take a look at your own life. Look at it over a long period of time. Look to the way back in the back when and look to the now. Yes, I am certain you have grown older and maybe become more mature and perhaps even more calculating in your thoughts and actions but on the inside of your inner being, the who you truly are, how much of that has really changed?

Have you ever associated with a person who behaved in a specific way with some other person and you believed that they would treat you differently? But, when push came to shove they reacted to you in the same, very unconscious manner as they had to that other person?

Have you ever interacted with a person who has done some bad things either to other people and/or to you? But, they told you they have changed, that they would never do that again. But, that was a lie—perhaps not a conscious lie but a lie nonetheless. They ended up doing the same damaging thing that they promised they would never do again.

For a person to change in life is virtually impossible. People are who they are. You are who you are. Even if you can get the appropriate training and learn various coping techniques, it is still you choosing to intact or not intact those coping techniques. You are still you on the inside.

Think about your life. Think about the way you have acted towards other people. Think about the actions you have taken to get someone to like or love you. Think about the actions you have taken when you have tried to hurt someone. No matter what your motivation—no matter how true or how pure you believed your motivation to be, what you did was solely based upon what you felt. You were you doing what you wanted to do.

Look to your life. How much of what you think or feel has actually changed over the years of your existence? How much of what you do, based upon your thoughts, has actually changed? Have you changed at all? And, if you believe that you have, is that the truth or is that simply a lie you are telling yourself?

I Just Do Not Know What
Some People Are Thinking
04/Nov/2019 04:21 PM

Art is a very interesting thing. It is interesting because it is so personal. There is the artist who creates it and then there is the everyone else who it encounters.

Every artist, myself included, creates art as they feel it. For them, it is a projection of what they envision in their mind broadcast to the material world. Then comes the judgment. The judgment of like and dislike. That's natural. Due to our programming we all like what we like and dislike what we don't like.

For most artists, myself included, they create art because it is something they must do. Art is everything creative: painting, drawing, photography, music, poetry, writing, acting, filmmaking, you name it. As long as it is instigated with the vision of generating something new, different, personal, and unique, than it is art.

Most artists, myself include, create art and they hope others with like it and appreciate it. Most artists, myself included, put their art in a format that may be viewed by the world. But, we do not force it down the throat of anyone! If someone wants to check it out; great! If not; all good.

Some people, however, do not possess a clear understanding of how personal-art may affect the life of other people—affect it in a way that they do not want. They make other people encounter their art when other people do not want to encounter it. Though you could argue that is still art, art inflicted on someone else, who does not want to encounter it, only creates negativity.

There is this Starbucks that I go to all of the time. It is situation just above the ocean so it provides the customers with a great view while enjoying their coffee and their conversation. This afternoon I go there and as I am waiting for my latte to be created I notice that there is a guy out on the Starbucks' patio strumming his guitar. Okay... That's a first...

The guy looked to be in his early fifties. He had greying, brown hair that was a bit long and a beard. He wasn't homeless or anything. His clothes were clear and he wore them well. Visually, by the way he dressed and his hair, he reminded me of someone you may have seen in the 1970s.

I stood there waiting inside. I kept noticing people getting up and leaving.

Anyway, with my drink competed and my very good (highly recommend) bag of Starbucks popcorn in hand, I walked out the back door and onto the patio to grab my seat. Immediately, I could not help but hear the guy's guitar playing...

Now, I hate to be critical (because art is art, right?) but his playing was really bad. And, his guitar was out of tune. For a musician, like myself, that just drives me nuts. But, there he was strumming along to the obvious discomfort of many, including me.

Was he doing anything wrong? No, not really. He was just embracing his art. But, it was art that I just could not be controlled by. Like others, I got up and left.

I don't know... Maybe that guy time traveled from the 70s where that kind of stuff was acceptable. ☺

This is the thing, for all of us artists, you do what you do, you create what you create, maybe it will be loved, maybe it will be hated but you must give people the space to come to it on their own and never force it onto the life of anyone because forcing your unwanted interpretation of art onto anyone only creates a world where you drive everyone away and you are left sitting alone on a patio where no one is willing to sit next to you.

I've Written a Lot of Things for a Lot of People
01/Nov/2019 08:53 AM

Recently, I was contacted by the editor of this Tantra-based website asking me if I would be interested in writing for them. The editor had read an article I have up on this site that I had written about Tantra Yoga. They told me they liked it.

Throughout the years I have made much of my income via writing. I've written a lot of things for a lot of people. Once upon a time I wrote a lot of stuff for magazines and you could pick up my works on the newsstands. Newsstands... Do they even exist anymore? A lot of my stuff has also been published by academic journals. As that stuff is very case-specific, it is a lot harder to find. But, if I have a basis in the subject, and I am asked to write something, I am happy to do it.

For anyone who knows me, or has read my poetry, prose, or novels, you know I have a basis in the Tantric arts. Throughout my life, and via my writings, I have attempted to integrate that understanding into the more mundane areas of human existence and, dare I say, physical aspects of life. Back in the day when the headlines would state that the singer Sting would have sex for ten hours, as he was a practitioner of Tantra, that kind of stuff just made me smile. That's Tantric kindergarten people...

Me, I was lucky enough to study with some true Tantric masters in Khajuraho, India when I was in my early twenties. So, I have a fairly substantial basis for my understanding about Tantra, the Tantric arts, and Tantra Yoga.

In any case, I received the aforementioned request, via email, and I read it on my iPhone.

When I read it, I had a very specific idea about what I would probably find when I checked out their website. I get home, turn on the Mac, and in association with the other stuff that was going on, I pop over to their website. Surprise! It was not at all what I had expected.

First of all, it is a very well designed website. But, the first thing that you (I) notice about it is that they are offering female out-call and in-call services. I popped through the photographs and the women are beautiful. I mean they are all really gorgeous. The website details various mentions about Tantra. It even has a few very well written articles about what to expect via one of their Tantric (sexual) encounters. Interesting... The whole thing made me smile.

Now, I have no way of knowing if the women they provide are actually trained in the advanced practices of Tantra, nor do I have any way of knowing if the people who contact these women, and book an appointment with them, are actually interesting in delving into the enlightenment that Tantra is designed to provide. I have a guess but it is only that, a guess.

Tantra, Tantra Yoga, and even the physical/sexual Tantric experience that has been much touted in this modern era is specifically designed to raise the practitioner to a higher level of metaphysical understanding via very specific techniques. But, look around you, look at your own life, look at the life and the mindset of those people you know, how many of them truly care about walking a pathway towards enlightenment? How many of them truly care about encountering the higher realms of human existence? Now ask yourself, how many of them care about having sex with a truly hot lady?

Anyway… That's the situation and that's the question—your koan for the day if you will…

I send a note back to the editor asking about the specific of writing for the site. Would I do it? Of course. If the price is right. Hell, read my novels and you will see that I am not scared by the dark side of Tantra.

The biggest realization I gained from all of this is the proof that all life is maya—it is an illusion. It is what people put out there and what people expect all based upon personal desires while pretending it to be something else.

You can get what you want. You can even pretend it is something other than what it actually is. But, at the heart of living a true life and encountering samadhi you must know who you are and what is true, even if you pretend that it is something else.

Hey, here's my first article for the site. ☺

Here's a little meditation technique for you...

Right now, wherever you are, take a look at the clock and mentally note what time it is. Now, close your eyes and Stop. Freeze your mind, stop your thinking, and stop your movement. Catch yourself.

Take notice. What are you feeling? Study your body very well. Take note if you are sensing a pain, an itch, a tingle, an anything...

Once you have clearly defined what your body is feeling, move to your mind. What are you feeling? What emotions are you encountering?

This meditation technique is not designed to force yourself to stop thinking and concentrate on a mantra or anything like that; it simply allows you to totally embrace your moment. Do that.

Freeze your mind in this moment. Define a clear mental picture of what you are feeling and what you are mentally experiencing. Once you do this, allow your mind to wander. Where does it take you? Consciously witness this progression.

In some cases, depending on your current state of mind, you may find your mind going to the trial and the tribulations of the day. Perhaps you fade into a fantasy. Or, if you are in a passive state of mind, you may fade into encountering abstract images like when you are falling asleep. Whatever the case, do not judge your physical and mental sensations, simply witness and take note of them.

Perform this mediation technique for a long as you can hold your mind in a passive, intuitive state. When you can no longer do this, open your eyes.

One of things that you will no doubt realize when practicing this meditation technique is that time will have slowed down immensely. When you open your eyes, though you may have gone through a number of vivid mental images, perhaps you will still be in the same moment as when you closed your eyes or perhaps only one minute or two will have passed.

This meditation technique will provide you with a deeper insight into Your Self in any given moment of time as well as it will allow you to chart how once you enter the meditative mind time finds a new definition.

Admit That You Are Nothing
29/Oct/2019 05:01 PM

The majority of most people's lives are spent in pursuit of something: becoming something, getting something, or possessing something. The majority of most people's lives are spent dreaming about what they desire. The majority of most people's lives are lived attempting to obtain that which they will never obtain. The majority of most people's lives are spent in a state of dissatisfaction because they are not all that they want to be or that they do not possess all that they wish to possess. Due to the factors, the majority of most people spend their entire life in a state of discontentment, displeasure, disappointment, and frustration.

What if you accepted the fact that you were nothing? What if you did not attempt to achieve anything? What if your life was not defined by your desiring to become something? What if you simply admitted that you were nothing? Wouldn't everything become a whole lot easier?

In Zen Buddhism there is the concept of, *"Wu."* Wu means, *"No thing."* Not, *"Nothing,"* in the sense of something. But, *"No thing,"* in the sense that everything has no absolute validity.

In Zen Buddhism there is also the concept of, *"Sunyata,"* Sunyata describes the fact that all things are empty. That all things have no absolute essence; they are simply a projection of the mind.

Think of your life. Think of all the things that your desires have lead you to do. Think of all the pain you caused to the life of other people and to your own life due to the pursuit of your desires. Think what your life and the life of other people would have been like if you did not walk down the path of desire.

Think of all the things you have done; the actions you have taken and the money you have spent in order to become who you wanted to be and in order to own all that you wanted to possess. Think what your life would have been like if you had not done those things and spent that money.

Becoming nothing is the easiest thing in the world. You just surrender to the fact of nothingness. You do not have to do anything. You simply submit. By submitting you become. In fact, if you do submit to the nothingness, in Zen Buddhist understanding, you have become the ultimate example of life. Yet, how few people desire to follow that path?

Can you embrace the no-thing-ness? Can you re-embrace your ultimate essence? If you can, all things fall into place; your life and the world become perfect in their simplicity.

Try it. Even if you do it for a moment here or there you will gain vast new understandings into the ultimate truth of your existence.

The Things That People Do
29/Oct/2019 08:14 AM

Watch the news, listen to the stories that people have to tell and it is pretty amazing the fucked up things that people do to one another. Whether it is the obvious actions of killing, beating, raping, or stealing, down to the more subtle realms of the people who are pissed off at a person or want to hurt their life (for whatever reason) and do thing like release revenge porn, text them to kill themselves, or tell distorted truth or lies about them... ...There are a lot of things that people do that can really hurt another person.

Due to the volume at which we hear many of the bad things that are done to others, most of us focus on those really big bad deeds. But, look around, look at your own life, there are all these things that go on in each of our lives—the small things that truly affect us is some negative manner and/or hurt the people we know. The lies someone told, the unsubstantiated, misconstrued facts that some felt they had the right to reveal, onto someone doing something based on only thinking of themselves and not taking you or anyone else into consideration: the noisy neighbor, the rude person driving on the street, the person who lies, the person who smokes in public, the individual who throws trash on the street, and so on.

All of this stuff gets done as a means to hurt or control the life of someone else but what does it prove? It proves the benefit is only in the mind of the individual who is leashing the hurt and gaining some sense of something by hurting that someone else.

I think of this couple I know... They were together forever, more than twenty-something years. Through hell or high water I thought they were going to tough it out till the end. Then, out of nowhere—at least nowhere to anyone but them, they got divorced.

You always hear stories about the woman getting big alimony payments but in this case it is the guy who is getting paid the palimony. He got to keep the house, he got half of the bank accounts, (bank accounts that were solely contributed to by the wife), plus he gets paid half of whatever his ex makes forever. Forever! This, when he has a job. I bet a lot of divorcing couples would like to met this guy's lawyer. But, what he is doing is a chump move. It makes him look like less than a man. But, to him, he scored. Scored, big time. He's living good on someone else's dime. I can only wonder what their kids, (who are still very young), are going to think about this man when they get old enough to understand. I am certain they will be very disappointed with their father.

Does this man care? I doubt it. If he did, he wouldn't be doing what he is doing. In fact, I am told, he said he wants his ex to hurt. But, she did nothing wrong. No cheating, just working. I can only imagine the karma he will eventually encounter.

Now, I am not trying to psychoanalyze these two people. I couldn't do that because nobody knows the true inner-workings of any relationship but the two people involved. What I am saying is think about it, once there was love. Now, one person is knowingly hurting the life of the other and taking her to the cleaners as the old saying goes. If a once married-person will do this, think about how the people who really do not hold any interpersonal love or time-spent with a person will behave. Think about the things they will do to mess with the life of someone else. Thus, meet the birthplace for all hurtful actions.

There are also so many people out there who really try to help others. There are people like the firefighters who are out there on the lines of life and death at a moments notice. ...The police, the military, the doctors, the nurses, and the EMTs. There is even the person who cares enough to care and says something nice when other people are embracing negativity or picks up a piece of garbage that is damaging the landscape. There are a million examples of people who do good things but it is generally only the large scale actions that are broadcast at a volume that will be heard by the majority rather than understood and appreciated by the very few.

Just as the previously described interpersonal melodrama details the bad that people are willing to do on a personal level, motivated by personal reasons, most good and positive deeds are only done on a scale that affects the limited number of people involved. Think about your own life. Think about the things you remember when someone came to your aid or your rescue. Think about a time when someone did something special for you. Think about a time when someone said something nice to you. It may have been a small thing, at least by the standards of the greater whole of the world, but that small action, that kind word made everything in your everything just a little bit better.

What do you think is better, living a hurtful life that damages the existence of others while creating ongoing long-term karma for yourself or only embracing the good, the caring, and the conscious?

It is you who decides how to feel the way you feel about anybody. It is you who decides what you do towards anybody. It is you who sets your destiny into motion by what you think, leading to what you say and what you do based upon how you feel.

Are you in control of yourself enough to control your actions and only say and do good things? Or, do you allow yourself to do self-motivated, hurtful things?

Good is good. Bad is bad. There really is no in-between.

Who do you want to be? The person who does good or the person who does bad? What you decide to do will forever define the rest of your life.

Blaming Others Instead of Blaming Yourself
28/Oct/2019 09:21 AM

How often do you blame other people for situations that are taking place in your life? How often does your mind go to thinking about what some person has done to you that (as you see it) negatively affected your life? How much time do you spend blaming that other person, in your words or your writings, as you are in communications with others? But now how about this? How much time do you spend thinking about the people that you have hurt in life—the people who feel you have damaged their life?

Some people live in a world of blame. They live their life, like we all do, but they focus on what other people have done to them that has held them back (as they see it) from accomplishing all that they wished they could accomplish. In fact, for some, this is one of the main focuses of their thinking mind. They continually ponder about what others have done to them. How about you?

Take a look at a time in your life. A time when you feel someone messed with you and it hurt your life. Really bring it clearly into focus. What did that person do to you? Spell it out in you mind. Okay, once that situation is very clearly defined in your mental focus, think about this, why did they do it? Why did you allow them to do it? What factors did you contribute to that relationship? And, how much of what happened was all or partly your fault for you deciding to be in that relationship in the first place?

Do you ever consider that factor as your mind is going towards casting blame? Do you ever think about how you personally contributed to the creation of that relationship and why it took the turn that it did?

It is easy to blame. But, how many people who do the blaming actually take the time to study their fault in the creation of any life-situation?

Now, let's turn this around a little bit. Think about a person who blames you. Think about a person who feels you have hurt their life. Take a moment and really think this through. Get a clear mental picture of what you did, what your doing did to them, and what were the results of your actions on their life leading to the blame that they focus on you.

What did you do? Did you hurt them? Did you hurt their life?

Why did you do it? When you were doing it, were you thinking about the impact it would have on them, as a person and on their life-evolution, or were you only thinking about yourself?

Some people are very selfish. Some people only think about themselves. This too goes to the sourcepoint of blame. When they do something to someone else they don't care about it or the consequences. Have someone do something to them, however, and then all of the focus of their blame is expounded towards that person, many times in a pattern of lifelong broadcasts.

In life, we are all going to be hurt by other people. A good person tries to never hurt anyone. They certainly never attempt to hurt other people intentionally. If they do hurt someone by accident, they attempt to fix any damage that they have created. Not everyone is like that, however. Many people are very selfish and very self-serving. If they hurt someone they lie and deny—they never accept any responsibility. They make excuses and seek justifications for their actions. But, that never takes away the pain that they have caused someone else.

It would be nice if no one hurt anybody. Perhaps the more one retreats from the world, the less chance they have of being hurt. No hurt equals no potential for blame.

But, what can you do with blame if you are feeling it or if someone is focusing it on you? That's a very personal question and the answer varies by each situation.

If someone is focusing it on you, care enough to care about that person's feelings and do something to fix it. That is the right thing to do. Do you care enough to care? If you do that becomes the definition of your life. If you don't that too becomes the definition of your life.

If you are in a state of blaming it is really you who must find it in your own being to remove that blame as a defining factor of your life. If the person who hurt you is not actualized enough to accept the fault and attempt to try to fix what they have done to you or your life, no level of blaming them is ever going to change their mind. Plus, no level of blaming them is ever going to make you feel any better. Blaming will simply become the defining factor of your life.

There is no easy answer if you find your life has been hurt by someone else. But, the one thing that you do not want to do is allow that person to maintain control over your life longer than is absolutely necessary. Every minute, leading to every day you focus on blaming them, you give them control over your life. Let go, move on, do not allow them to maintain control over you and your thoughts by focusing on that negative thing that they have done to you.

In closing, some people do bad things. Some people will intentionally do things that may negatively affect your life. Sure, this hurts. This creates anger. But, the longer you allow that action to remain a central focus of your mind, the longer that person's negative actions control your life. Move on. Stop the blame. Never let them hold control over your tomorrow.

You Wanta Make a Movie?
26/Oct/2019 11:37 AM

I've been professionally in the film game for about thirty years. In that time I have witnessed a lot. There has been a lot of changes in technology, audience reception for films, and the attitudes that people bring to the table when they wish to become part of a project.

I have met some really great people in association with filmmaking. People who are a pleasure to be around and great to work with. I have also met a lot of not so nice people—people who bring their own weird agenda to the table and/or do some really uncool things on and off of the set. But, that's just the nature of the beast.

One of the main things I have realized, in all of these years of filmmaking, is that most people do not want to partake of the craft. Sure, many-many people have dreams of being a filmmaker but very few step up to the plate and actually conceive of a project, learn how to actualize it, and follow it through to completion. There are a lot more people who simply want to walk on a set, spit out a few line, and walk away a star. That's great! Good for them. But, not many of them are going to get very far in their quest.

Being based here in Hollywood, there are all of these people who come here with the dream. I have spoken about this subject in a lot of my articles and books on the subject. Many of them believe that if this certain famous person could do it, so can they. Sure, that's a great belief to have. Unfortunately, of the literally millions of people who come here, maybe one in that group makes a name for themselves. The rest are left going to auditions (if they are lucky enough to get an agent) for roles they will never get or being an extra.

All this being said, early on in my emersion into the film business I realized that the true art of filmmaking is behind the camera. Actually creating the film. There you possess some control over what is actually being produced. There, at least you can create a something, as opposed to hoping for something to be created around you.

Throughout my years in the film business, I have actively tried to help other filmmaker actualize their dream. I offer people crew positions when I have them available. I give them advice when they ask me for it and so on. I have even offered to create a movie with some people who seem to be very driven. But, what I have experienced more times than not is, even the person who really talks the game, even the person who really expresses the desire, even the person in film school, when push comes to shove and I say, *"Let's make a movie,"* they always find a reason not to. What happens to their career? I don't know. They never do anything. But, the reality is, it did not have to turn out that way. They could have joined forces with me (or anybody else) made a movie and got their name out there.

Sure, as stated, there have been a lot of people who have worked with me over the years. They did something with their filmmaking dreams. They achieved something. But, there have also been so many more that have not.

Yes, yes, periodically people ask me to finance their films. But, I don't do that. I have seen way to many people take money from whomever and never finish what they started. Dreams and promises mean nothing in this business.

As a personality, I am frequently asked to be an actor in other people's films. Like I always semi joking tell them, *"The only bad movies I'm in are my own."* But, the truth is, I am an active member of the SAG/Aftra Union so I cannot be in a nonunion film—which most indie films are. But, I am asked by the people who are already out there doing it. They are living their dream. They are actualizing their creative vision. If they ask me to help them behind the scenes, I am happy to do. And, that's the thing, particularly in the realm of indie filmmaking, you help each other out. From this, new realities of cinema are created.

So, what am I saying here? …Particularly in this day and age, there are filmmaking opportunities everywhere. You can make a movie with your phone! You simply have to have the fortitude to actually do it. Sure, dreams are great. But, if you don't make your dreams your reality then they are nothing more than something that is locked inside your head. …Lost forever inside of your brain.

If you want to make a movie, make a movie! Reach out to people that you believe can help you and get it done!

All creation is art. It doesn't matter if it is loved or hated by the masses. Who cares what they think? The only criteria is, if you get it done, it becomes a something and from this you have become something, a creator.

Create. Make art. Make Cinema.

*   *   *

24/Oct/2019 01:38 PM

Most people who believe that they are helping
others are doing nothing more than feeding their
own ego by performing a job where they receive
thanks, admiration, or respect.

The People You Don't Want To Meet
24/Oct/2019 08:32 AM

Have you ever had one of those experiences where someone comes up to you and starts a conversation and you can just feel they are bleeding bad vibes and/or negativity? Then they shake your hand or something and you wish you had some sort of psychic antibacterial gel that you could wash off the goop they just laid onto your life.

In life, all people are who they are. In life, most people are defined by what they are defined by. In life, most people are pretty much middle of the road. You may like them. You may not like them. You may like what they think. You may disagree with what they think. You may like what they believe. You may believe something else. You may like the way they look or how they dress or you may think they look foolish. But, that is all just the projection of the internal onto the external.

Again, most people are pretty much middle of the road. If they enter your life you are fine with that. If they are not in your life, that's okay too. But, then there are some people that just over-project. What they bring to the table is so overpowering that it just makes you feel yucky.

Each person chooses to project what he or she wishes to project to the world. Each person chooses to speak what he or she chooses to speak to the world. Each person chooses to dress the way they want to dress and to encounter life in the way they wish to encounter life. But, most people do this from a perspective of unawareness. Sure, we are all products of our childhood and our environment but it is what we do with those influences that define us as who we are and who we become in life. Some people are just negative or weird and in some cases/many cases they do not even realize that is what they are projecting outwards to the world.

What do you do when you encounter someone like that? How do you behave towards them? For me, I think the best thing to do is to always be nice and be positive. I smile. I compliment them. Then, I move along. That is not to say that I am not left with some level of wishing I had not interacted with them but, at least, I hope, their interacting with me will give them just a little bit of something positive to refocus their energy upon.

I have met people who have spent their entire life based in a mindset of negativity. You can see this has projected into what they have encountered in life. They are down on themselves—down on where they work, what they do, and whom they interact with. The thing most of these people never realize, however, is what they have projected onto their own life. They are the embodiment of their dissatisfaction and they move it forward day after day, year after year. As they are the source point of this negativity, it will never leave them.

You can see this in the way a person dresses. Look to the people who are dissatisfied and you will see them dressing in a very scruffy, disheveled manner. Maybe their hair is always a mess. Their car, if they have one, will more than likely be old, broken, and messy inside. This is the same with where they live. The external is always a projection of the internal for any person.

I remember I was once having a problem with my plumbing. A couple of plumbers came over to fix the issue. I got to talking to one of them, a young Mexican-American man, and I mentioned that being a plumber must be a pretty good job as, at least here in the States, they get paid pretty big dollars. He said it was a good job but I could sense his negativity about his profession. He went on to state that whenever he went out to eat lunch at a coffee shop or restaurant everyone looked down on him because his clothing was so dirty. I suggested why don't you bring a clean polo shirt along with you everyday and change into it when you go to lunch. It was like a massive bolt of enlightenment had been provided for the young man. He could do his job but do it without receiving the sour looks of the masses in the restaurants.

This is the thing about life and those who embrace negativity... Chances are you are not going to change them. You can try... You can say good things. You can compliment them. You can even give them suggestions about a better way to live their life but it is only that one in a million person that it going to receive Satori from what you have to say.

The things is, you've got to try. Sure, you may not have wanted to meet that person in the first place. Sure, you do not want them to remain in your life. Sure, you do not want to be gooped by them on a daily basis. But, if you do not pass on that one little bit of positivity nothing in their life will ever change.

How much time do you spend delving into your Deep Mind? How much time do you spend peering into the recesses of what truly makes you who you are? Most people glaze over the understanding of Self by filling their time and their thinking mind with tools of distraction. Whether this is via reading books, listening to music, watching TV, surfing the internet, being consumed with their daily activities, daydreaming about their desires, thinking about their family, their job, or praying, very few people choose to dive into the silence of the Deep Mind.

Whereas most never even ponder their Deep Mind—the why they are who and what they are, others question the logic behind investigating the deep regions of their Being. Sure, some go towards psychotherapy but that is more motivated by dissatisfaction with life than a quest for Inner Knowledge.

The fact is, if you ever aspire to get to the Inner Reaches of the Essence of who you are and why you are you, you must choose to transvers the obvious constrains of your reality and move into your Deep Mind.

How do you track into your Deep Mind? Though there is no one technique the first and most obvious one is that you must define your Deep Mind. This is not hard to do. We all know where this place of Inner Consciousness is and we have all visited it from time to time. Most, however, simply never develop a relationship with this space of Inner Being and, in fact, turn away from it when they randomly encounter it generally at times of going to sleep and/or waking up.

The Deep Mind is at the base of your Being's harness to reality. It is at the space just between Consciousness and the Divine. It is at the seat of your concept of Self.

How do you consciously travel to it? There is no one technique but the one I like is one that was taught to me Pir Vilayat Inayat Khan when he was instructing a small group of people and myself when I was about sixteen. What he suggested one do is to visualize a small light in the blackness of the mind and then follow that light into the deep reaches of your mind. Though this process begins by visualization it allows you to travel deep into the Deep Mind as by imagining that light taking you back farther and farther you can access parts of your Inner Consciousness that you may not travel to simply by meditating or thinking.

Many ask, what does one hope to do by exploring this region of their True Being? There is no one answer but by traveling to the depths of your Deep Mind you will come into contact with the You that You truly are. You will come to understand the Inner Workings of your Essence and you will emerge with a deeper understanding of the mystery of all that is your life.

Like all techniques of Higher Consciousness, accessing your Deep Mind is a developed and ongoing understanding. As it takes time for you to separate from your Thinking Mind, which provides you with the illusion of how you should think and feel, practicing this technique grows through time and developed understanding.

Most people only want to see what is in front of them. They only want to believe what they believe to be reality. They base all of their definitions and desires on what they believe to be real. But, if one does not peer into the Inner Workings of Personal Reality they can never truly know who they are, why the are, and what is the ultimate meaning of their life. Take the time to explore your Deep Mind.

Take a moment right now. Think about it a little bit, and come up with a definition, *"I am a..."*

For most people there will be more than one thing that will come to mind when they clarify this definition. They will be able to clearly state that they believe they are a this or they are a that. That's fine. That's natural. But, in this moment right here, right now define in your own mind who you believe yourself to be.

Most people possess a random definition of themselves. Many people, however, never really think about this definition. They simply pass through their life doing what they are expected to do and though what they do makes up all of the days of their life they never come to a clearly defined realization about why they are doing what they are doing, why they have chosen to do what they do, why they choose to do what they do, and why life has given them the set of choices they were allowed to choose from. Thus, they do not know who they truly are.

Many people define themselves, at least in part, by their occupation. In fact, some people are almost wholly defined by what they do to make a living.

In some cases, people are very proud of their job. In other cases, it is simply something they have been forced into and are forced to do on a daily basis. In either case, via loving and/or hating what they do, many people think of little else because so much of their life is defined by the time that is involved in their occupation.

Many people hope to become something more in life. Many people struggle and strive to become something more. Many people study to become something more. Many people lie to become something more. But, just as one of the clearest truths of life is, you never know what something will actually be like until you arrive; the projection of what many people believe they will achieve is quite different from the actual reality of what something truly is when and if they ever get there.

Think of all the relationships that go south and the person is very sorry they ever got involved with that other individual in the first place. Think of all they businesses that fail and the person is sorry they lost all of their time and their money hoping to establish that business.

Those are simply a couple of very obvious example but look to your own life, where did you hope you would find yourself at this stage of your life, where do you hope you will find yourself in the next stage of your life, and what are you doing to get there? ...Look back through what you have already lived, do you believe that dream you currently hold will actualize in the same matter that it is envisioned in your mind?

There are a few reality-based TV shows on the air these days that go into the businesses of people that have mismanaged their companies and are about to go under. In one such show a man and his team goes into bars and retrains the staff and completely remodels the establishment. At the end of the show they usually detail how the bar is now making more money.

Living in the Los Angeles area, where several of the bars featured on this show have been located, I have witness, (though not intentionally), how virtually all of the bars featured on the show very quickly went under or another management team took them over after they failed. Thus, the gift(s) these people were given were not understood, cherished, correctly used, or appreciated. Proving, people are who they are. Yes, they can want something better. Yes, they can want something more. Yes, they can dream. But, even if they are giving that substantially helping hand in achieving their goal they will still fail because they do not possess the mental wherewithal to truly understand human desire in association with reality-based consciousness. They want what they want but they do not hold the rational and intellectual advancement to actualize those dreams into a substantive reality.

How about you? Is how you define yourself, is how you have lived your life defined by unfulfilled desires, roads that you believe that you should not have taken, and damaged caused to you and others by a pursuit of your desires and your livelihood? Or, has your life been a pathway of conceiving and then achieving while providing for yourself and giving to the life of others?

Desire is always a double-edged sword. It invokes wanting and it involves achieving. But, what is the achievement of your desires going to cost you and what is it going to cost others? What has the achievement of your desires cost you and what has it cost others?

Most people take very little time defining who they are, why they are, and truly understanding what they hope to achieve. From this, comes a life defined by random chaos and no sense of understood arrival at each step of the evolution of a person's existence.

If you do not truly understand who you are and why you desire what you desire, you can never achieve anything of any substantive value in your life. At best, all you will have lived is a life designed by random wants that have lead you to nothing more than spending your Life Time defined by no more than occasional moments of happiness or sadness.

If you want to be more, you really have to be more. Being more begins with understanding your reality and comprehending your destiny. All this begins by truly knowing who and what you are and what you can actually achieve.

*   *   *

20/Oct/2019 08:09 AM

Sometimes you have to make a big mistake to know what to never do again.

The Lack of Evolution
18/Oct/2019 09:56 AM

Humanity is broken up into two distinct groups of people. The first keep an open mind, continually trying to advance themselves in knowledge and understanding, and believe that they evolve as they pass through their lifetime. The second group is defined by the person who is locked into a mindset of stagnation: they know what they know, they believe what they believe, and they are content to pass though their life with whom they consider themselves to be. Neither of these two groups of people necessarily chooses to be defined by these categories but through personality, upbringing, or karmic destiny they simply find themselves in one of these two groups. Meaning, you are who you are. No matter what you believe yourself to be, your life is, nonetheless, pretty much a case of predestine programming.

Most people feel like they have changed as they have passed through their life. They feel that they grow, learn, and that they evolve. But, is that truly the case? Have you actually become anything different than what you were five, ten, twenty, or thirty years ago? Yes, your body has become older. Yes, you have lived what you have lived. Yes, maybe you have learned how to control your emotions a little bit better. But, have you truly changed? The immediate answer from most people to this question is, *"Yes, I have changed. I have become better and I have evolved."* But, just because you think something, that does not make it true.

Do you keep a journal, writing down your life experiences and your feelings? I believe this is a very important thing to do throughout your life. Whether you do this via writing, tape recording, or video taping, what this does is that it allows you to look back to the who you used to be in the long ago and the far-far away. It gives you a chance to witness and remember what you were living, thinking, and feeling back then.

If you have this as a tool, right now, step back ten years ago or so. Look, read, listen, and see what you were thinking and feeling. How much different was what you are living now compared to what you were living then? How much of what you are feeling now is different from what you were feeling then? How much of how you are acting on those feelings is different from how you were acting on those feeling back then?

If you have this tool, and if you access it, you will immediately witness that though you have perhaps changed your life in certain manners, who you were is still who you are. Though specific elements of your lifestyle may have changed, you will still be defined by that internal you that projects itself to the world and understands and interacts with life in a very specific manner.

Most people do not keep journals (by whatever technique or definition). If you don't, take a moment right now and pick a point in your life— maybe ten years ago or so. Find one of those specific points in your memory that you actually remember very clearly. Now, close your eyes, take a few moments to travel back through time—take yourself to that place; really feel it, truly remember it. What were you living then? What were you feeling then? Who were you then? What type of person were you? What type of things did you think? What type of things did you do? What type of behaviors did you exhibit? If you are honest with yourself, you will most likely conclude that very little has change in how you think, feel, and encounter life.

So, what does this tell us? It tells us that most people are locked into a very specific pattern of encountering life. It does not matter if you consider yourself a spiritualist, an intellectual, or a bigot, who you are is who you are and though you pass through life collecting new experiences, who you are never really changes.

In life, interpersonal change only occurs when a person either chooses or is forced into that change. But, what does that change actually change? People can believe all that they want that they are growing and evolving, but learning new skills or even following a new religion is not an evolution it is simply encountering and learning new stuff. The person inside does not change. The person inside, at best, simply has learned something new.

So, next time you believe you are on some evolutionary path of realization, look to who you truly are; look to what you think, how you think, and how you interact with the world. Have you really changed? Have you really evolved? Probably not.

As the storytelling always begins, once upon a time…

Once upon a time I knew this filmmaker who was really at the crux of the independent film game at one point in history. What he did was to get money from investors and then he would make action-adventure movies in which he was the star. He would hire really established actors to be in his movies, to gain an audience and generate sales, but he would put his name above theirs. Great ploy, I thought. As he was paying their salary, he could do whatever he wanted. The rest of the cast and the crew he would pay very little or nothing.

He was a great hustler. And, I am saying that as a compliment. He would get money from wealthy investors, make his movies, and he lived pretty well.

This went on for a while until he had screwed over one to many people. People would even do things like call up my agent to see if I knew where he was. …Not that I would tell them even if I did but that just goes to show how what he did affected someone like me who had nothing at all to do with his business dealings. I was told at one point he even had a contract out on his life from messing with the wrong people in Vegas. Finally, after being sued by so many people and so many companies, he went bankrupt and lost the rights to all of his movie titles. After this, he would try to get acting gigs and find investors and the like but the world had changed, the video/digital revolution hit and everybody was making their own movies. He never got back on his feet, at least not in terms of the independent film industry. I would look at his webpage and stuff like that every now and then and nothing too much seemed to be going on.

Skip forward a decade or so and now he is a religious influencer on YouTube. He has thousands of followers and people who are watching his talks. People are giving him money as he speaks about fire and brimstone, damnation and salvation. The only problem is, listen to his talks and you can hear the insincerity and bullshit in his voice. He speaks with the same tone as he did when he was acting or hustling investors back in the day. As I know him, I know that is not how he actually speaks. Yet, he has found a new cult of people who are willing to pay to listen to his jibber jabber.

Certainly, there is nothing new about this style of religious extremism and the preachers who disseminate it to the masses. Recently, an interesting TV series was presented on HBO, The Righteous Gemstones which really shows a lot of the nonsense that takes place behind the scenes of the religiously wealthy. But, look to any church, anywhere in the world, and there you will find believers and people who need to believe. Enter, the preacher… Maybe that should be the title of his next film. ☺

Anyway, most of us out here are fairly whole onto ourselves. We have our families and our jobs; we have our beliefs and our superstitions. But, we live without being motivated and dominated by the words spoken by a person who claims that they have some knowledge and an understanding that we do not possess

We are all unholy. We are all impure. Most of us, however, do not claim that we are something else and that we have a message that should be heard. Most of us do not make our living by taking passages from the scriptures and altering them to activate the fears of the masses in order to stimulate people to give us money.

Now, I am not criticizing this man or any other so-called preacher or religious teacher. We have all had teachers in our lives. And, if nothing else, they show us what not to do. What I am saying is that the people who seek religion, due to there being something lacking in their life, are such an easy target. This is what those (that style of) religious teachers preys upon: the venerable, the lonely, the unfulfilled, and the lost. From my perspective, that is just wrong. Sure, all of these teachers will claim that they don't make anyone listen to them or give them money but they all know there are people who will. And, instead of giving these people the tools to be complete, to find their own pathway to grace, understanding, and enlightenment, all they do is guide them into disciple consciousness and to come back for more because that internal stimuli is all they have to make their life feel not so empty and unfulfilled.

What can we all learn from this? I don't know... There's a lot of things... One, know who you are listening to. Know their past. Know who they used to be and what they used to do. Two, sure listening to someone is invigorating; it may even be stimulating and fun, but is that how you want to live your life—guided by the thoughts and the religious interpretations of someone else? Three, if someone is making their living by quoting the scriptures and using religion as the cornerstone of their livelihood, you really have to question, why? Why can they do that, and you give them money, when you have to check in everyday to the nine-to-five?

I don't know... I have nothing whatever so ever against the person of which I speak. In fact, once upon the time, I liked the guy. What I am saying is that it seems to me that he's just playing another role. ...Another role where he is hustling people and taking money from people as a means to perform and put his name above the other, more notable, actors. ...He's not the only one... So, think before you listen. Think before you give. Think before you believe.

It is always enlightening to watch the mind of people and how they project their inner demons onto the world. Whether this is done via arrogance, criticism, anger, violence, or demeaning behavior towards other, if you look, if you listen, you can always find what a person's actions are motivated by.

In this recent era, particularly in the Western World, there has been a lot of talk about the resurgence of White Nationalism—racism by any other name. But, has it ever gone away? Look to any race in any country in the world and you will find racism. Be it Black against White racism in South Africa, Asian against White or Black racism in the various Asian countries, Hispanic against other races in the Latin American countries, or simply White against Black or Black against White racism in the U.S., xenophobic ideology is everywhere.

But, why is that? What it truly comes down to is that many people have no sense of accomplishment or Self and, due to this fact, they grab onto whatever is readily available to them. *"I am White, you are not." "I am Black, you are not."* From this is born a world defined by hate crimes driven by nothing more than the color of a person's skin.

Look around, you will see it everywhere. The things people write on the internet for no reason but to hurt someone or something and/or to cause controversy with the hope of stirring up the emotion's of others. Listen and you will hear it all around you; every time a person gets mad at someone for cutting them off when they are driving or bumping into them as they are walking down the street. Hate filled emotion, often driven by race, is one of the common denominators of modern society.

Certainly, race is not the only tool used as a means to dispel an individual's inner demons. Religion is another one. The position one finds themselves in society is another defining factor. But, the fact is, people look to what they already have as a means to use that something against another person when they are not whole, complete, and fulfilled within themselves.

If you look to the life of a person who has accomplished something—something outside of themselves, there you will find a person who is more focused on that something and moving towards a new something than the need to find a distraction via hate—hate by whatever means is available to them.

But, how does one get to that place in their life where they embrace hate? Due to racial, cultural, national, and financial demographics many times a person allows himself or herself to be solely controlled by where they find themselves in life. They allow the defining factor of their life to be placed upon them by unchosen circumstances.

Indoctrination into how one is going to live their life begins at birth and becomes more clearly defined as the years of their life progresses forward. Who one associates with and what one does, based upon those associations, form the factors of how one thinks, how they process life, and how they project those influences out to the world. Though certainly not everyone is defined by where they were born, the race they were born into, and the

304

socioeconomic factors that defined their early years, many are unable to escape these elements, and from this, they become frustrated with their life, leading to bad, hateful behavior.

Education is one of the best methods to escape the factors of negative indoctrination that one may be born into. Yet, many people do not seek out this pathway. In fact, many of the people who preach the gospel of hate proselytization against mental advancement. By keeping someone locked in the fray they are then allowed to possess control over that individual. And, this is what many people who embrace a hate-filled mindset desire, they want others to experience what they are experiencing and from this not only find a means of releasing their angst but to feel they are somehow in control by criticizing and injuring the life of someone else and/or damaging that something else, while gathering those of like-mind around them. Look to any person who practices criticism and hate, what do they desire? To hurt other people and to gain followers who agree with them to make them feel whole and that they are contributing to the expansion of whatever it is they believe. Though the person who embraces this lifestyle is most likely not self-aware enough to realize this, that is what is taking place.

Again, let's go back to education. Education is everywhere in this day and age. The problem is, much of this education is based upon a hate-filled mindset. Look to all of the people who find websites where people expound hate speech. Moreover, look to all of the people who do this is a very sublet fashion via critiquing the life and the works of others. Look to the people who focus upon writing negative reviews about products, and the list goes on. The fact is, all negativity equals is negativity. All hurtful, hateful speech equals is damage. And, if you anyone, you hurt everyone.

When I was an undergraduate, in my junior year at the university, I had a professor who said a very profound thing. He said, *"Going to college teaches you how to think. It doesn't matter what you are studying but by pursing a degree you learn how to think."* I have always found that to be very true. For example, a trade school may be a great place to learn a work skill but it does not teach you how to think. It is only when you are forced to study subjects that you (maybe) do not really want to study that you are forced to embrace and learn new ideologies. I think this is what needs to take place throughout one's life. You need to be forced to learn. With this, all of the negativity of self-motivate or propagandizing thought is driven from your brain. If nothing else, you learn how other people think and feel and, from this, you gain not only new understandings but compassion for the plight of all of humanity.

Sure, I know, college is expensive. But, what is the cost of your life? What is the price you are willing to pay to understand?

In closing, negativity and hateful speech and hurtful behavior are all around us. But, that does not have to be who we are. We can be different. We can be better. We can be the person who stops negativity at its source with compassion and understanding. We can be the person who says something positive when the other person is saying something negative. We can each be the vehicle for change.

*   *   *

15/Oct/2019 07:18 AM

Why do you only remember some of your dreams?

The science of meditation is often described as a pathway to achieving a higher consciousness and making the meditator a more passive and fully integrated individual. At this point in history most people have heard about the concept of meditation and a few have even attempted its practice it via a yoga or martial arts class they may have taken but few have sat down and actually attempted to truly meditate.

If we look around the world, at this point in history, what do we see? We see people with their face glued to their smart phones. Yes, virtually everything is available in that small device, linked into the internet, but is that meditation? No. In years gone past, people first found their way to handheld distraction via *Game Boys* and *iPods*. Before that it was the *Walkman*. Before that it was newspapers and books. Yes, all of these tools serve a purpose but are they meditation? No. Do they cause a person to rise to a higher level of human consciousness? Most likely, no.

If we look to early points in history, people often claim that meditation was easier in simpler times. Yes, times were simpler; there were not so many millions of distractions. But all life, at all level, is often confounded with predicaments and problems, no matter at what period of time a person has lived. There has always been distractions and reasons for people not to meditate.

The fact is, few people, throughout history, have ever decided to meditate. And, that is what meditation is defined by, a person's choice to decide to meditate. You cannot force a person to meditate.

The greatest factor that causes a person not to meditate is they do not see the need. Does it equal more money? No. Does it equal receiving the desire they desire? No. So, why do it? In fact, certain religious traditions warn against it. They claim it is a way to let the devil in and claim his domain over your mind.

All that aside, even for the person who has attempted to meditate, they will clearly define that it is not an easy process. It is not easy to silence the mind. Due to this lack of ease, numerous techniques have been developed to cause a person to possibly meditate in a less demanding format. The Zen Buddhists developed numerous physical techniques that were designed to incorporate movement into the silent mind. *Kinhin,* walking meditation. *Kyūdō,* archery. *Ichigo,* tea ceremony. *Ikebana,* flower arranging. And, the list goes on. Even Transcendental Meditation (TM) was designed to teach a person how to meet the silent mind of meditation for a very short-lived period of time.

All of these methods are fine but do they truly introduce the practitioner to the silent mind? Do they truly allow them to meditate? Of course, this is debatable. But, the fact is, the essence of meditation is for the practitioner to meet the divine essence of being via a completely silent mind and anything that is not complete silence is not true and actual meditation.

So, where does this leave the person that wants to meditate? Where does this leave the person who has tried to meditate but realizes that thoughts continue to come to their mind?

Meditation is not hard. Meditation should not be a struggle, nor should it be a reason for the meditator to chastise themselves for not being able to keep their mind silent.

My suggestion is to meditate wherever you can, whenever you can. Instead of only forcing yourself to get up during Brahmamuhurtha, at 4:30 AM in the morning, and sitting to meditate, as they do in the ashrams—instead of forcing yourself to sit in full lotus posture, meditate anywhere, wherever you can. If you have a moment at home, sit or lay back on the couch, release your mind, and meditate. If you are on a bus or an airplane, close your eyes and meditate. If you are somewhere beautiful, scenic, and peaceful, close your eyes and meditate.

Even if your mind releases itself from the reality of reality and enters a space of silence for a moment, you have achieved meditation. You have touched the essence of your being intermingling with the absolute. The more you do this, the more you will understand the true essence of meditation and the more you will be able to come to that place of Pure Mind.

Meditation does not have to be and should not be hard. Simply meditate whenever and wherever you can. Meet the absolute.

12/Oct/2019 01:29 PM

Along as a person is affected by some negative something that you did to them you will forever be defined by that karma.

11/Oct/2019 12:27 PM

Many people speak about the benefits of meditation. They are missing the point. Meditation has no benefits. It is the pathway to supreme nothingness.

If you think about yourself before you think about the life of another person all you have done is to make this world that much more selfish.

*   *   *

11/Oct/2019 07:06 AM

There is no such thing as a secret. There is just certain things that you don't know.

The Things That Are Lost and Long Forgotten

In each of our lives we possess a set of memories—things that we knew that happened because we were there. But, how many of those things does anyone else know about? Sure, the other people that were there may know about them but that is about it. Meaning, there are very few people who know anything about the life you have lived and the memories that you possess.

For some, this is a good thing. They don't want people know about what they did what back in the way back when. In fact, they lie about their past. But, does a lie ever change the truth? Maybe... If no one knows, then no one knows. But???

On the other side of the issue, some people spread their life story all over the place. This is particularly the case since the dawning of the age of the internet. People put their autobiography out there all the time—what they are doing, what they are thinking, how they are feeling, and what they are seeing.... But again, is it always true? I think not. There is a lot of embellishing and lying going on.

But, more than simply what people say about themselves, there is a quest for knowledge. Some people (few people) really want to find the truth of the origin of the all that is. From this, they seek and they study. But, when all the history that is now so readily available is clouded with self-promotion, falsehoods, and lies, how is it possible to even find the truth?

The thing that sent me to thinking about this was when someone recently asked me about the fact that my father once owned a restaurant. As the story goes, after his service in the military, in World War II, he came home, saved up his money, and opened a restaurant near the U.S.C. campus in the early 1950s. He developed it and it became very popular.

In my early childhood, I have so many memories based around that restaurant. But, now they are just my memories. Everyone else is gone.

Anyway, after my father had a heart attack he decided that he would retire early so he sold the restaurant to two, then very famous, football-playing brothers. At the time, I am told, it sold for more than any restaurant had previously sold for in the history of L.A. The brothers quickly resold the restaurant, however, to another local female restaurateur, after one of the brothers went into a coma due to a football injury he incurred while on the field.

I actually went into the restaurant one more time when I had just tuned twenty-one, the legal drinking age here in California. The Dalai Lama was giving a lecture at the nearby Shine Auditorium, on his first trip to the U.S., and I thought I would stop in and grab a beer. I know, I know... It's a little weird to drink a beer before going to see the Dalai Lama but it was once my father's restaurant and all...

The inside of the restaurant had remained very much the same as I remembered it. Overall, however, it was just a very weird experience for me as my father had passed away just a couple of years after he sold the place. Anyway...

In any case, the restaurant remained very popular until, due to city redevelopment, it was closed in the 1990s.

I rarely think about that restaurant. But, as I was asked about it, I gave it a quick internet search.

What I found was that all that is referenced about it is the female owner. No mention of my father who opened and developed it. No mention of the football-playing brothers who bought it from him. Nothing... All that history is gone.

I am sure if you go into the city records of Los Angeles or something you could find the original business license and stuff like that. But, who would even think to do that if they didn't know the history of the restaurant. In fact, who does that? Who takes that kind of time to actually do their research. Most people just search the web. But, the web is full of self-promoting deceptions and historically inaccurate facts. People lie!

Like the blog I wrote a few years ago, *"I am the last person who remembers my father,"* most of our histories are simply going to disappear. Certainly, all of our memories will be gone when we are gone. ...Memories that were and are so important to us but to no one else.

What does this tell us? I don't know? I guess most of us are just fucked. For all that we lived, all that is important to us, is only important to us. All our memories of the life that we lived are only held in our own mind, because no one else cares about them.

So, live while you live because it's all that you have. Remember while you can remember, because no one else will. And know, when you looking for the truth in history, most of what you read will simply be the self-serving bullshit put out there as a means to make something or someone appear to be the way that someone else desires it or them to be seen. ...The history you read is rarely a history based upon the memories of what actually took place, told by the people who were actually there.

09/Oct/2019 07:17 AM

What does having a fantasy actually prove?

08/Oct/2019 08:21 AM

When you wake up in the morning do you ever take the time to greet the sky, embrace the air, acknowledge a bird that is flying by?

08/Oct/2019 07:23 AM

If you ask someone for something, and they give it to you, you will forever owe that person.

If you take something for someone, without their permission, you will forever owe that person.

Your life is based upon the destiny you create by what you do.

Simply because you receive what you want, in any given moment, by taking or receiving is not the ultimate definition of your life.

There will always be a price to pay.

* * *

08/Oct/2019 07:20 AM

Most people think about the things that happened to their life that they didn't like.

Few people take the time to think about the things that didn't happen to them that could have been catastrophic.

Everybody possesses an illusion about the people that they know of but do not actually know. This goes for the greats of history from Buddha to Jesus onto political and religious figures down to movie stars, music stars, reality stars, authors, artists, and sport's players. People believe that they know what that person must have been thinking and why.

People talk about and discuss what that other person must have been feeling. They give discourses on why that person did that something that they did. They write books about the life of these people. But, the fact of the fact is, if you do not personally know someone, if you have not personally interacted with that someone, you have nothing to base your suppositions upon. Even if you have read something that they have written or heard words that they have spoken, via some form of recording, you can never know what caused them to write or to speak those words. Therefore, everything you are saying about them is most likely false. This makes you a liar.

Why do people focus their thoughts and their words on the life of someone else? There are a number of reasons for this but the most prominent ones are, they want to seem like that they know that secret something about that person that no one else can know or that they have some deep realization about that someone that everyone else needs to know.

A certain breed of people are constantly focused on the life, the deeds, and the actions of that someone else. Again, there are numerous reasons for this but the end result is that no matter what notoriety a person gains by speaking of that someone else all they have done is to bring attention to the life of that person and they have done so in an untruthful, biased manner.

Look at your own life. How much time do you spend thinking about that someone else. Whether it is one of the grand life figures of history or the person in your classroom who you have a crush on, when you got to know them, if you got to know them, was anything that was concocted in your mind valid? Was it real? Were they who you thought they were or were you surprised to find out who they truly were; what they thought and what they were willing to do?

Now, think about you. Think about the people who thought that they knew you but were totally wrong. Maybe they described you to other people. Maybe they explained the reason behind your life actions, or how you think, leading to what you do and why. How right were they? How wrong were they? Did they truly know you at all?

We each live our life as best as we can live it. We each do what we do based upon what we think, predicated upon how we were programmed to encounter life. But, our life is our life. We know our life. Can we ever know the life of someone else— especially that someone else that we have never met?

It is easy to fall into a pattern of following the illusion of life. Believing but having no true experiential basis for that belief. But, all that leads to is a life based upon illusion. What is illusion? It is life deception. It is a life based on a lie.

So, the next time you find yourself thinking about and speculating how and why that other person, that you never met, is thinking what they are thinking, leading to what they are doing and why, stop yourself. Realize that you have no basis for your conjecture. The next time you find yourself speaking about that someone you never met, stop yourself. Realize that at best all you are speaking would be a lie because you do not and can never know why they think what they think leading to what they have done.

Stop living the life of illusion. Know yourself and you will find that is the only one you truly need to know.

*   *   *

05/Oct/2019 08:55 AM

When you say you are doing something for somebody else who are you really doing that something for?

326

* * *

04/Oct/2019 04:54 PM

What did you do for yourself today?

What did you do for god today?

You Weren't There So You Don't Know
04/Oct/2019 08:53 AM

Have you ever had the experience where someone begins to tell you something about yourself—something about what you did or didn't do in a particular situation? …They are there telling you how you did behave or how you should have behaved but they are basing their entire discourse simply upon what they heard about the situation either from you or from someone else. When I encounter those situations I want to scream, *"You weren't there so you don't know!"*

For some reason, certain people decide that they know what another person should or should not do. For some reason, certain people decide that they know what a person has lived better than the person knows them self. We could go into all kinds of ego-based and psychologically motivated reasons why certain people behave in this fashion but the fact of the fact is, no one can know a person better than they can know themselves. No one knows what a person has lived or experienced better than that person knows that experience themselves.

For each of us, there are life experiences that we wish we could change. There are life experiences that we wish would have turned out differently. There are life experiences that we wish we would have said or done something differently. But, we did what we did and we are left with what is left.

The fact of life is, no one knows the what never was. Sure, in our minds we play out scenarios. We fantasize about what could be and what could have been if only we had handled a situation differently. But, the reality of reality is, we played our cards as they were deal to us the best way that we knew how to in that moment. To second guess ourselves may be a common and a natural occurrence but it never leads to that moment, lived back then, to have been lived any differently. What was, was.

For some reason, certain people wish to place their appraisal onto the life situations lived by other people—telling them what they believed they should or should not have done. For some reason, certain people wish to judge the life and the life choices of that someone else. Why do they do this? Ego. They believe they know better how a person should have lived their life better than that person knows himself or herself. But, do they? Or, do they simply find it easier to judge the life of someone else rather than to judge themselves in a critical and constructive manner?

As we pass though life we are all going to encounter situations where we wish we would have done something differently. As we pass through life we are all going to see people making choices and taking actions that we believe they should not. But, at the essence of any true life is the realization that each person must live their own destiny, based upon the choices they make, even if we believe they could have and/or should have made a different choice.

So, live your life as best as you can. That's all any of us can do. But, never judge the choices and the frame of mind of that someone else because the fact of the matter is, you can never truly know what that other person was thinking or feeling that has caused them to make the choices that they have made which resulted in the life they lived in any particular situation. You weren't there so you don't know.

03/Oct/2019 12:11 PM

Do you ever watch your shadow walking?

*   *   *

What happens when you turn around and the sunset
is gone?

Think About How Much Life
You've Lived Since Then
03/Oct/2019 09:07 AM

I was being interviewed recently and, as always seems to be the case, the interviewer brought up, *The Roller Blade Seven*. ...Sure, that's great! I'm glad that for whatever reason that movie has remained in the minds of the masses for all of these years. But, realizing that this guy was fairly young, I asked him how old he was. *"Twenty-eight."* My response to his question, *"We made that movie almost thirty years ago. That was before you were even born. Think about how much life you've lived in your twenty-eight years of existence. Think about how much life I've lived since then."*

Many people hold onto a point or a period of time in their life. They do this for whatever reason. For some, something great went on back then. For others, it was something horrible or they did something wrong that came to define the rest of their life. But, the thing about life is that it goes on. Everyday something new and different happens. Sure, a lot of the days fade into the mundane. But, there is always something new and revelatory going on if you open your mind to it. There is always something different, great, and inspirational if you allow it to come into your life.

For me, RB7 was one of my first films. Don's been dead fifteen years or so. I have made so many movies since then. Sure, many of them are relatively obscure but they are out there, they can be seen. My cinematic evolution can be charted but how many people take the time to do that? They just want to hold me to the past. Everything about my life and my filmmaking has evolved since then.

RB7 was a long time ago. Yet, people lock their mind and their impression of me into that point in time. I don't!

The main thing to keep in mind, as you pass through life, is that everything you do creates who you are and how you will be perceived by the world. In fact, some people work at projecting a perception of themselves to others—whether that perception is the true them or not is always a subject open for debate. But, all that self-generated perception and all that imposed definition from the mind(s) of someone else, is not you. You are you. Only you know you. Only you can be you. Only you can live you. So, don't let yourself be locked into who that other person thinks you are. And, do not attempt to place definitions on other people because inevitably you will be wrong.

Live your life because this is all you've got. Don't become stagnate. Live new. Do new. Become new. Evolve. And, never be held back by your past.

*   *   *

02/Oct/2019 05:04 PM

What did your today equal?

The Gift That Never Gives
and the Interviews That Never Happen
01/Oct/2019 09:00 AM

I always find it kind of interesting that there is a certain group of people who pursue knowledge out there and really delve into the mind and the mindset of a particular individual. Of course, there are also those who see something or hear something and have their mind already made up. But, that's sad I think, because those people never allow themselves to step into the brain of someone else and see things through the perspective of that other person.

For me, I enjoy reading and/or watching interviews with a person who has lived a certain something. They always have something to say. Sure, sure, a lot of people lie or exaggerate in an interview situation—or try to make themselves look like a certain kind of something, but that too is interesting as it provides interesting insight into the mind of that individual.

One of the most interesting things that occurs during the process of an interview, at least for me, is when I had a certain something to do with a situation: be it a film, some music, a book, I know the filmmaker or the martial artists, or whatever and the someone who is telling the something is telling stories that aren't really valid or truthful. ...Maybe they didn't really understand what was going on or why. Maybe they just misinterpreted the situation. Maybe they just want something to sound better and/or more than it was. Maybe they just want something to sound worse than it was. Whatever... But, once a something is put out there people believe it, even if it is wrong. Then what? I always find that, *"Then what,"* interesting.

People form the process of their lives by what they see, what they hear, what they do, and whom they interact with. They create the next step in their life by the words of others and the creations of others that they encounter. One thing leads to the next and the next...

For some, they encounter a tidbit of information, provided by someone, they then believe it and it causes them to take that next step in their life. But, what if what they heard is not based upon foundational fact? What if what they hear causes them to act in a manner based upon a misprojection of truth and reality? Or, what if what a person hears is simply misconstrued and misinterpreted by that listener in an erroneous manner? Then what? What does that mean to the life of that person and what does that mean to the life of everyone else as each word, each action experienced by someone else, causes all those others who heard or see it to move forward with what they do next?

Sometimes people come to me, via whatever means, and actually ask me questions. Cool! I always try to answer. Some people come at me with questions based upon an attack scenario, however. They want to pick a fight based upon asking a question. I always find that ridiculous. That's why, though I am always happy to answer questions about my whatever, I often turn down the interviews. ...Interviews proposed by people to make a name for themselves, based upon the life someone else (i.e. me) has lived.

But, more often than not I have found that most people don't even want to ask me the question(s). They just want to project their own appraisal onto my life and my creations. They think they know, but they do not. And, I am just using, *"Me,"* as an example, because that kind of stuff goes on all over the place.

Do you ever wonder why you think what you think about a person or a creation? Do you ever ponder the questions you would ask someone—that someone that you are thinking about? Do you ever ponder why you would ask that question in the first place? Do you ever wonder why a person is who they are and why they do what they do? Or, do you already have your mind made up?

How you encounter life, how you encounter people, how you think about and speak about other people, and what it causes you to do, sets the stage for the entire evolution of your life and the progression of the life of all those who hear you.

Who do you think about? What do you think about? Why do you think about it? Do you ever think about that?

What you hear equals what you think. What you say, based upon what you think, causes you to do what you do? What you do causes other people to do. How much of what you think, leading to what you do, is based upon you and how much of it is based upon what you think about others and why you think other people have done what they have done?

As I always say, if you want to know the truth, go to the source. Ask and actually listen to the person who is at the foundational birthplace of whatever it is you are thinking about. From this, if nothing else, you can gain their interpretation into the reality that they have created. With this information you will, at least, be able to step forward and project your interpretation of your projection of someone else's reality with a bit more validity.

Never think you know until you know.

You Are a Fat, Ugly, Bald...
30/Sep/2019 01:08 AM

"You are a fat, short, ugly, bald, retard, white man, who lives with his mother, and doesn't have a life."

I was walking out of a restaurant in WeHo a few weeks ago and two people were having this heated argument. The words and the insults were flying until the one man said the previous.

Not really knowing what went on to send this discourse into action, a few of us onlookers looked at one another pondering what to do next. The man who had been hurling the insults turned and walked away. A moment or to later the other man walked away.

Intense... Those words were intense... But, as intense and as Politically Incorrect as those words were, think how many people throw insults at other people in much the same manner every day. Some do it face-to-face. Most do it behind the back of the other person or on the internet—which is the most cowardly way possible. But, look around you... Look at your life... Look at what you have heard and look at what you have said. How close to those words have you personally spoken?

My entire life I have witnessed as people have insulted other people. Whether it was very intense, as the aforementioned experience, or much more subtly, I have heard insults unleashed. But, the thing is, whether they are intended to critically hurt the person or simply spoken by a person believing that they have the right to provide guidance or to critically critique the life of another person, all words spoken in this fashion do nothing but damage.

As I have spoken about many times in the past, as a young child, growing up in South Central Los Angeles, it was commonplace for people to call me, *"Honkey,"* or *"White Paddy."* When I reached my adolescent years, in East Hollywood, the Latin populous commonly refereed to me as, *"Pinchie weto,"* or, *"Freak,"* because I had long hair. And, the oncoming physical attacks and/or the fights, based on that mindset, were an expected commonplace occurrence because I stood out. I always had to be ready.

In fact, my parents and their friends sometimes used racial slurs. Even me, as a high-schooler, I remember using now inappropriate terms to describe those who were attracted to the same sex. I did this as a means to define my placement in reality and to establish my manhood. Now, I realize how stupid that was. Yet, it was a sign of my times.

So, what does this tell us about life? What does this show us about life? It explains that most people have not evolved very much. The same words are spoken to hurt other people that should have been left behind decades ago. And, no matter what the motivation or the justification that a person believes is theirs to unleash words of judgment, criticism, and insult, all it does is to diminish the person who is speaking those words because it shows them to be nothing more that a person attempting to unleash hurt onto the life of someone else.

Sure, some people feel that they have the right to say whatever it is they want to say. Sure, some people feel that the other person has done or said something that offended them. Sure, some people feel that they know more and/or are more than the person they are casting the insults towards.

But, are they? Are they really? Or, are they simply just another insecure person attempting to make themselves look like something more by attempting to diminish the life of that someone else by saying words designed to hurt them?

Think about who is saying what and why.

Everyone is a Human Being
27/Sep/2019 09:24 AM

Whether it is a guy hoping to hook up with that pretty girl he sees or a woman believing that she has met the man of her dreams—or even somebody who meets someone that they believe will help their life or their career, people view other people through the lens of physical desire. ...They see something that they want and they go after it.

The opposite is also true. People see someone that they believe to be unattractive, (for whatever reason), and they turn away. Maybe they even make snide comments or jokes about that person.

But, here's the question... Is that individual, who is seen as undesirable, any less of a human being?

People place an enormous amount of weight on physical appearance. People place an enormous amount of weight on the where a person exists on the spectrum of financial and occupational success. People place an enormous amount of weight on externality and what they desire in that other person's externality. How about you? Who do you desire to be in the presence of and why? Who do you seek out and why?

The fact is, though much of this life is dominated by external appearances and the desires other people place on the external projection of someone else, this externality is not the essence of a person nor is it their ultimate definition. If the only people who can succeed in life are the physically attractive then what of all of the other people on the planet? And, who sets the absolute definition of beauty?

Moreover, if the only people who are deemed worthy of following are the already successful, then where are the new/next revolutions in ideas formulated?

Everybody is a human being. They each have feelings and they each have a contribution to make.

Many people forget about this. This is why there is so much hatred in the world. This is why there is so much turmoil. This is why so many people are damaged by the words and the actions of others—damaged simply because they are viewed by that someone else to be something lessor.

Be more than that. Embrace everyone no matter what they look like or where they find them self in the financial pyramid of life. Understand that they have feelings too—they have hopes, they have dreams, and they have a contribution to make.

27/Sep/2019 09:20 AM

Most people do nothing for anyone but themselves.

They think of themselves, attempt to make their life better, care only about who and what they care about, associate only with those people they want to be around, and only pray for themselves and those they care about or love.

*　　*　　*

27/Sep/2019 09:19 AM

A person only needs you as long as they need you.

You Will Never Understand Their Culture

Whenever a people are taken by a new and different culture or a tradition, particularly if it is a religious tradition, they try to emerge themselves within that tradition. They attempt to become part of that convention. This is particularly the case over the past century or two when the Eastern Religions found their way to the West. They were so unique and they promised a completely new take on how to engage in life and interact with reality. From this, many Westerners attempted to engage in these religious and become a practitioner. Though there is certainly nothing wrong with this, as it allows a person to expand their mind and perhaps gain new insight into life and reality, when one was not born into a culture and/or did not live that culture from birth, they can never truly understand that culture. Thus, no matter how much a person claims to be a This or a That, they are not.

From the beginning of the New Age forward, there have been teachers and self-proclaimed prophets that have taken hold of the words and the wisdom of these distant teachings and have attempted to package them for the Western mind. Some have become completely submerged into these traditions, while others have studied them from a far. In the twentieth century and forward, people like Allan Watts and Ram Dass are ideal examples of people who attempted to present these traditions in a way that could be consumed by the Western Mind. These two, and many-many others attempted to learn and then explain these teachings. But, no matter how far they submerged themselves into the outward physical practices they could never truly understand the essence of these religions. Why? Because their internal diagnostics were formulated in a completely differently culture with a completely different frame of reference towards life, god, reality, and spirituality.

All a Westerner, who thinks that they are a yogi or a practitioner of Hinduism, has to do is to walk into a Hindu temple in India, observe the way the people worship, and they will immediately realize that what consumes the mind of those believers is vastly different from what is propagated by books and teachers who gear their teaching towards the Westerner.

Just as person who was raised in a strict Hindu tradition, in a county like India, may wish to embrace Christianity, they too will be missing many of the essential elements of internal make up to actually practice this religion as it was meant to be observed. Yes, they may believe. Yes, they may pray. But, the essence of their being was created with a different set of foundational elements, and from this, no matter how hard they try to be a Something, they cannot.

People play dress-up all over the place. Go to India, go to Thailand, go to Japan, (and even in America), you will find people wearing the clothing of various traditional religious sects that they were not born into. Maybe they believe that they are that. Maybe they are fooling themselves. Maybe they are attempting to fool others. But, the fact of the fact is, what you are not, at your deepest essence, you can never become.

Study, learn, experience, find your own perfection, all that is great. But, never fool yourself into believing that you are something that you are not.

Do You Ever Wake Up
and Realize You Were Dreaming?
17/Sep/2019 07:46 AM

Do you ever wake up and realize you were dreaming? Have you ever had the experience of maybe you were laying in bed on sitting back in a comfortable chair and you doze off and you enter into a very vivid dreamscape where you are totally one with and a part of your dream? Then, maybe it is a noise outside or maybe something jars you awake and you realize that you were simply dreaming and not actually living the dream reality that you were, only a moment ago, totally a part of?

As we live our lives, we live an accepted reality. In our dream, however, as real as they may feel, anything can happen—you can feel and do virtually anything. While you are existing in that dream, it is very real. But, you cannot stay in that dream forever. The absolute fact of dream reality is that you are going to wake up.

Now, let's think about your life. Have you ever had a belief that you really believed in—a belief that guided you to live a specific reality? Maybe it was on the smaller scale of reality— maybe you really liked an actor, a music group, a sports player, a priest, a minister, or a politician. You liked them but then time when on and with that time you changed your mind. What happened to that feeling about that someone out there? Did they change or did you change? And, why did you stop believe in the reality you once held so close?

On a more personal note… Maybe you liked or loved another person. But then, something changed. Maybe they did something to you that you didn't like, maybe they starting hanging out with a different crew, maybe they shunned you, or maybe you simply realized they were not the person you thought them to be. From this, all the beliefs you had in and about that person were eradicated.

The opposite could be true, as well. Maybe at one point you did not like a person. Maybe you thought you had your reasons. But then, you got to know them and you changed your mind. You did come to like them. Did they change or did you? What made you change your mind about them? Were they actually any different? Or, did your desired perception of them simply change? And, is that their fault or is that your fault? Whose reality were you basing your reality upon?

Or course, this concept of perceived perception and projected—believed reality goes to all aspects of your life. But, think about this, while you are living, whatever it is your are living—while you are feeling, whatever it is you are feeling, do you ever question the essence of the reality that you are living? Do you ever ask yourself, why you are feeling what you are feeling? And, do you ever come to terms with the fact that what you think you are living is not based in reality at all—it is simply based in your belief about the reality you think you are living?

The fact is, most people never question their reality. They live what they live what they live. They believe what they believe they believe until possibly something radical happens and they finally possibly change their mind. Or, they do not. They just live what they live until they live no more. Then, they and all they believed—all that they thought they were living is gone.

Your life is based upon your perceived reality about what you are living. Your life is based upon what you think about what you believe. But, what makes what you believe a truth? What makes what you think you are living a truth? Isn't it simply what you think that you are doing?

But, look to your life... Look to the people and the things that you once believed it. Look to the things that you once based your entire existence upon. Look to the things that are gone. Where did they go? Why did they go? Isn't where they went and why they went all based upon your changing perceptions of that something or that someone out there? Thus, it—the all and the everything is simply based in you and what you believe. But, obviously what you believe is not truth and it is not reality because what you believe changes.

So, what does this tell us? It tells us that we are all, at best, living a dream. We are living what is locked inside our own heads. Yet, we project that interpersonal mind stuff out to reality with our loves, our hates, our expressed feelings about the whomever and the whatever, and our desires for things to be the way we want things and other people to be.

This style of thinking—this style of living is all very disingenuous. It is all so self-motivated. It is all based upon the dream that we believe we are living. But, when we wake up, that dream is gone. We realize that we were simply living an illusion. An illusion that dominated what we were thinking, equaling what we were saying and doing, and how we were behaving. Is that how you should live your life?

Most people throw their Life Time away until they are up against the wall of death and then they say, *"Whoops."*

16/Sep/2019 07:12 AM

How much time do you spend thinking about how
what you are doing is affecting someone else? How
much time do you spend caring?

16/Sep/2019 07:11 AM

The average person doesn't care who gets hurt as long as they get what they want. How about you?

"I'm an artist, goddamn it. I don't have to rationalize, justify, explain, or defend anything that I do!" This is a mantra that my *Zen Filmmaking* brother, Donald G. Jackson, and I would joking exclaim whenever we encountered some type of nonsense in the process of filmmaking.

For anyone who is actually an artist, they will immediately understand this statement. For anyone who is not, they will not, as they do not possess the creative understanding that inhabits the mind of an artist.

Art is the heart and the soul of every culture. Art is what defines a people and a culture at a specific point in history. Though everyone knows about art, few people actually spend any time thinking about art and fewer yet are driven to embrace its essence and create art.

For some, they find their life purpose by discussing and defining the art that others have created. Are they an artist? No. At best, they are a historian. At worst, they are a critic.

It is kind of like the character(s) that you will often find in the films of Woody Allen; the know-it-all who wants to appear to be so intelligent, espousing their knowledge, telling someone/everyone about the who, what, when, where, and why about an artist and their creations. But, just like in the films of Woody Allen, this person is always exposed to be wrong. Meaning, you cannot define art. You can view it. You can love it or you can hate it. You can be inspired by it or you can be repulsed by it, but if you are not the creator of that art you do not possess the internal understanding to define that art.

I have spent my whole life creating art of one type or another. Many people have. One of the main things that I have witnessed, via the varying fields of art that I have worked within, is that very few people who seek to be artists, or claim to be artists, truly are an artist. Most simply imitate what they have seen created by others. Few actually possess the internal vision to push the boundaries of whatever genre they work within. This is why, at whatever period of history you look to, the art from that timeframe will be very much the same: be it painting, poetry, writing, music, photography, filmmaking, whatever... Few people have the unique vision to actually develop a distinctive style, refine that style, and then present that art to the world.

So, what does all this tell us about art and the artist? What it tells us is that, if you are an artist, be an artist. Embrace your art. Develop your art. Live your art. And, do not let the judgment of your art, unleashed by those who can never understand your art, hinder your life as an artist. If you are not an artist, that's fine; live and be what you are. But, if you are not an artist, understand that judging the mind of the artist, critiquing the motivations of the artist, criticizing the art of an artist is like trying to catch the wind; you can't. Because if you are not the sourcepoint of any artistic creation, you can never truly understand the essence of what drove that artist to create that art.

Do you understand the difference between opinion and fact?

Do you understand the difference between your opinion and a fact?

Do you understand the difference between belief and fact?

Do you understand the difference between your belief and a fact?

Do you present your opinions as a fact?

Do you present your beliefs as a fact?

Do you tell people what is your opinion and what is your belief verse presenting everything you speak as a fact?

One of the major problems with this world is that people confuse opinion and belief with fact.

One of the major problems with this world is that people believe opinion and belief to be fact.

Take Some Time in the Morning
13/Sep/2019 08:27 AM

When you wake up in the morning what do you do?

Are you woken by an alarm clock each morning?

Or, are you allowed to wake up slowly, roll around, think the thoughts that the new day brings, and finally decide to get out of bed when you feel that it is time to get out of bed?

Most people do not address a new day with any sense of consciousness. Many/most are woken up by an alarm clock, at a specific time, because they are expected to get up, get ready, and go to work. Many/most spend most of their life behaving in this fashion. Then, the weekend or the day off arrives and the person is typically too emotional strained and drained to do much else but wake up and restlessly roll around in bed, at about the same time as they are forced to wake up everyday, due to their biological clock taking control over their mind.

Even the person who lives in the ashram or the monastery is expected to wake up at a very specific time. They are then required to get up and meditate or pray.

For the people who wait for the weekend, they too often force themselves out of bed in the morning with little or no forethought, at a specific time, because they have, *"Plans,"* for the weekend—things that they want to do that they can't do during the workweek.

Though this is the status of most people lives, I believe that we all can see that there is something missing in this process. That, *"Something missing,"* is waking up and embracing the day with any sense of awareness or consciousness.

In each of our lives there is time when we naturally wake up. For each of us, this is somewhat different, but for each of us there is an internally natural time frame when our body and our mind knows that it is time to sleep and knows when it is time to wake. For most, however, this naturalness of sleep and wake is never allowed to guide the life process as the requirements of modern life are allowed to be in control.

The fact is, there is very little most of us can do about this fact. As an adult, or even as a young student, we are generally required to get up when we are expected to get up as we must make money to survive and/or go to school so that we can prepare ourselves to make money to survive. So, what does this tell us about life, what does this tell us about sleep, what does this tell us about waking up, and how can we do anything about any of it?

Here is the fact; most people do not attempt to live a conscious life. Most people never try to take emotional, psychological, or spiritual control over their life. They simply are dominated by their expected life and they live this way until they die. Though this is the commonality of a common life, it is does not have to be like that. You can consciously take control of your mind and your life patterns and bring them to a point where there is a greater state of expansive awareness.

To begin to do this, in regard to sleep and waking up, the next time you wake up take the time to consciously embrace the day—spend some time doing nothing; not jumping out of bed, not falling back to sleep, simply witnessing your mind, following your thoughts, studying your emotions and your expectations about the day, and coming to know what your waking up is truly about.

For each of us, when we wake up, the factors of the night of sleep are most with us. This is when we remember what we were dreaming, how those dreams made us feel, and what those dreams lead us to think about and realize. When we wake up, the emotions and the expectations of the day are most clearly in our mind. This is the time when we can study what we are feeling and why we are feeling it. We can even possibly clearly conclude, from a state of a clear and rested mind, what we should do next in our life to bring our existence to a better state of being.

Many/most people waste much of their life. They miss the opportunity that human existence is designed to provide. Waking up is one of those things that many/most people never take advantage of.

Even if you must be awoken by an alarm clock each day so you can get to work on time, choose an alarm that wakes you to the sound of the waves, birds chirping, or the wind in the forest. Don't force your self to embrace the day in a flash and get out of bed immediately. Wake slowly, naturally, take a moment and let your self meet the day with a sense of consciousness. From this, you may be allowed to embrace who you truly are and you may gain enhanced insight into what you should do to become who you can ultimately become.

Everybody Wants To Blame Somebody Else
12/Sep/2019 10:14 AM

Have you ever taken the time to watch the people in your life? Have you ever taken the time to listen to the people in your life? Have you ever taken the time to study yourself—what you think and feel and why you think and feel it? Have you ever taken the time to listen to the rumblings of the world around you? If you have, you will quickly come to realize that pretty much everybody wants to blame somebody else.

Whether it is a relationship that has gone bad, a bad situation in the work environment that has become toxic, or that something that somebody did not become, virtually everybody places the blame outside of themselves.

Think about it. Look at your own life. Look at what you have gone through and whom you have gone through it with. For everything that did not turn out the way that you had hoped, whom do you blame? Do you blame yourself or do you blame the other person? In most cases, that other person is the one who bares the brunt of the blame, at least in the mind of the individual who is doing the blaming.

Some situations of blame in life are very exaggerated. Some are kept on the more integral level. Whether that blame is yelled to the world or held as a well-kept secret, rarely does someone say, *"It was my fault."* Instead, all blame is commonly shifted away from any self-responsibility in the situation.

Take a look at your life. Take a serious look at where you find yourself in your life right now. Take a look back through time at what brought you to where you are right now. Who do you blame? Who have you blamed?

Think of something really bad that happened to you. Why did it happen? Was it solely the fault of that other person? Or, did you have a hand in instigating and/or creating that situation? If you did, why do you blame that other individual?

Now, think about the people you have encountered as you have passed through your life. Who blames you for what and why? Take a moment and think about these situations—those situations where you were interactive with somebody and that situation did not turn out the way that somebody else had hoped. Why do they blame you for the final outcome? Is that final outcome actually your fault? Ask yourself, was it actually your fault—the what went wrong? Is their blame valid or is it simply an exaggeration projection of their mind? Be honest. What elements of demise did you bring to the interaction and what components did that other person present? Clearly define who is at fault and why.

The fact is, in all life interaction two or more people bring two or more personalities and predetermined desires to any life interaction. From this, two or more sets of expectation are set into motion. In some cases, only one person emerges satisfied. In other cases, no one does. From this, blame is born but who is truthfully at fault? Is it the person who emerges happy at the end of the interaction to blame, simply because they seem to be the victor? Is that fair? Is that valid? And, what fault does the individual possess who holds the other person at fault?

In most life encounters two or more people choose to enter into the relationship—whatever that relationship may be. Sure, it is easy to blame the other person or persons if you emerge unhappy. But truthfully, where is your responsibility in your choice to enter into that life-interaction in the first place? Do you ever think about this? Do you ever blame yourself for you seeking out that life interaction? If you don't, you are very disingenuous with the reality of reality. In fact, you are lying to yourself and to the world.

If you blame anyone for what you chose to do, no matter what the outcome was, you are a liar—a lair not only to yourself but a lair to the world that you speak your feelings to. You chose to enter into that relationship. You chose to do what you did. Own your responsibility in that life situation. Stop shifting the blame from yourself and the entire world becomes a better, more honest, more real place.

THE ZEN